McGraw Hill

SOCIAL STUDIES WORKBOOK FOR THE GED® TEST

THIRD EDITION

McGraw Hill Editors

Contributor: Jouve North America

McGraw Hill

New York Chicago San Francisco Athens London Madrid
Mexico City Milan New Delhi Singapore Sydney Toronto

1 2 3 4 5 6 7 8 9 LHS 26 25 24 23 22 21

ISBN 978-1-264-25791-1
MHID 1-264-25791-0

e-ISBN 978-1-264-25792-8
e-MHID 1-264-25792-9

Contents

Introduction

How to Use This Workbook

This workbook contains practice problems to help you test your social studies knowledge and reasoning skills in preparation for taking the GED® Social Studies Test.

Start your social studies practice by taking the Social Studies Pretest at the beginning of this workbook. It will help you decide which chapters of the workbook will be most valuable to you. Take the Pretest in a controlled environment, with as few distractions as possible. If you want to closely simulate testing conditions, limit yourself to 70 minutes. When you are done, or when time is up, check your answers in the Answers and Explanations section at the end of the Pretest. Next, find the problem numbers you answered incorrectly in the Evaluation Chart to identify the chapters on which you need to concentrate.

Each of the four chapters in the book has dozens of questions on one of the four content topics that are part of the GED® Social Studies Test. The questions have also been carefully designed to match each of the following:

- the test content,
- the depth of knowledge (DOK) levels used to measure how well you understand each topic,
- the Common Core State Standards (CCSS) that you are expected to have mastered.

The exercises are not intended to be timed, but if you find that you are familiar with a topic, you could try timing yourself on a few problems, attempting to correctly work 5 questions in 10 minutes, for example. Answers and Explanations for the exercises are located at the back of the workbook.

Finally, when you have completed the last exercise, take the Social Studies Posttest at the back of this workbook. This test can help you to reevaluate yourself after practicing as much of the workbook as you feel is necessary. Answers and Explanations are located at the end of the test, and another Evaluation Chart is provided to help you decide if you are ready to take the GED® Social Studies Test or where you might need further practice.

At the back of the book, you will find a glossary of important terms to know for the GED® Social Studies Test. You can use this while you study or as a tool to help you review right before the test.

The GED® Social Studies Test

The GED® Social Studies Test is one section to be completed in 70 minutes.

The GED® Social Studies Test is a computer-based test, which allows for a broad range of item types. There are many multiple-choice items, each of which has four answer choices from which to choose. There are also many technology-based items with formats such as fill-in-the-blank, drop-down, and drag-and-drop.

- **Fill-in-the-blank:** These are short-answer items in which a response may be entered directly from the keyboard or in which an expression, equation, or inequality may be entered using an on-screen character selector with mathematical symbols not found on the keyboard.
- **Drop-down:** A list of possible responses is displayed when the response area is clicked with the mouse. These may occur more than once in a sentence or question.
- **Drag-and-drop:** Words are moved around the screen by pointing at them with the mouse, holding the mouse button down, and then releasing the button when the element is positioned over an area on the screen. Such items are used for sorting, classifying, or ordering questions.

About 50 percent of the problems on the GED® Social Studies TEst focus on topics in civics and government. About 20 percent of questions are on U.S. history. Fifteen percent of the questions address topics in economics, and 15 percent of the questions cover topics in geography and the world. As in the GED® Reasoning Through Language Arts Test, many questions require you to read and interpret a document. That document might be text, a chart, a graph, a diagram, or a map.

Visit http://www.ged.com for more about the GED® Test.

The Top 25 Things You Need to Know for the GED® Social Studies Test

Use this list as a guide for your studies. Be sure to study and practice each topic until you feel that you have mastered it.

1. **Types of Government:** Be familiar with various types of governments such as democracy, monarchy, dictatorship, and oligarchy.
2. **Independence:** Understand the reasons for and basic tenets of the Articles of Confederation and the Declaration of Independence.
3. **Creation of the U.S. Constitution:** Know the six basic principles that underlie the Constitution: popular sovereignty, limited government, separation of powers, checks and balances, judicial review, and federalism, and understand the compromises that were made in writing the Constitution.
4. **Citizenship:** Know the basic rights and responsibilities of U.S. citizenship.
5. **Bill of Rights:** Understand the reasons for the Bill of Rights and its contents.
6. **Amendments:** Understand the process of amending the Constitution.
7. **Branches of Government:** Understand the functions of each of the three branches of the U.S. government and how the system of checks and balances works.
8. **Elections:** Know the steps in the presidential election process and how elections are decided.
9. **Political Parties and Interest Groups:** Understand the function and influence of political parties and special interest groups.
10. **Colonial History:** Know how America was first discovered by Europeans and how the first 13 colonies were established.
11. **Revolutionary War:** Know the reasons behind the war; be familiar with important battles.
12. **U.S. Expansion:** Know the basic ideas of the Monroe Doctrine and Manifest Destiny; trace the westward expansion of America.
13. **Civil War and Reconstruction:** Know the reasons behind the war; be familiar with important battles; understand the effects of the war and the reconstruction effort.
14. **Industrialization:** Understand how the United States underwent industrialization and urbanization; know the effects of those transitions.

15. **World Wars:** Know the reasons behind U.S. involvement in World War I (WWI) and World War II (WWII); be familiar with important battles of WWI and WWII.
16. **United States as a World Power:** Explain the Cold War; understand how the United States became a superpower and what that entails in terms of foreign policy.
17. **Economic Fundamentals:** Understand opportunity cost, cost-benefit analysis, labor, capital, profit, productivity, and entrepreneurship.
18. **Markets:** Understand the relationships among price, supply, and demand.
19. **Macroeconomics:** Understand fiscal and monetary policies and the basics of international trade; define gross domestic product (GDP), tariff, inflation, deflation, and unemployment.
20. **Microeconomics:** Understand the law of supply and demand, banking, and credit.
21. **Maps:** Be familiar with several different types of maps, such as topographical maps, climate maps, political maps, and so on; understand how to read maps, legends, and keys.
22. **Movements of People:** Understand migration and push and pull factors; be familiar with migration patterns and population trends.
23. **Elements of Culture:** Understand what makes a culture unique (language, religion, ethnic groups, form of government, economic system, etc.).
24. **Political Ideas:** Understand liberalism, conservatism, socialism, nationalism, and Marxism.
25. **World History:** Have a basic outline of world history (see Chapter 4).

PRETEST

Social Studies

40 questions | **70 minutes**

This Pretest is intended to give you an idea of the topics you need to study to pass the GED® Social Studies Test. Try to answer every question, in a quiet area and with enough time so that you are free from distractions. The usual time allotted for the test is 70 minutes. Remember that it is more important to think about every question than it is to finish ahead of time. Answers and explanations can be found at the end of the Pretest.

Questions 1–3 are based on the following chart:

Principles of the U.S. Constitution

Principle	Meaning
Popular sovereignty	Power rests with the people.
Limited government	Government power should be limited, contained. Government officials must obey the rule of law.
Separation of powers	Executive, legislative, and judicial powers are distributed to different branches of government.
Checks and balances	Each branch has the ability to limit the power of other branches.
Republican government	Government is formed by officials elected by the people.
Federalism	Some powers are given to the federal government, some to state governments, and some to both.

Write your answer in the blank.

1. The Preamble to the Constitution states that "We the People of the United States . . . do ordain and establish this Constitution for the United States of America." This statement embodies the principle of ________________.

PRETEST

2. In 1920, the U.S. Senate voted against ratification of the Treaty of Versailles. What principle did this vote exemplify?

   A. checks and balances
   B. federalism
   C. popular sovereignty
   D. republican government

3. When the Bill of Rights was added to the U.S. Constitution, what principle was given greater strength?

   A. checks and balances
   B. limited government
   C. republican government
   D. separation of powers

4. Why does supply go up when new technology lowers production costs?

   A. Suppliers can make higher profits with lower costs.
   B. Demand for high-technology goods is high.
   C. Government regulation of the product decreases.
   D. Lower costs drive substitute goods out of the market.

Questions 5–6 are based on the following passage:

Between 1865 and 1870, in the five years following the end of the Civil War, a number of amendments were added to the United States Constitution. The Thirteenth, Fourteenth, and Fifteenth amendments are collectively known as the Civil War Amendments or the Reconstruction Amendments. These amendments were designed to provide equality under the law for the recently emancipated slaves.

- The Thirteenth Amendment, passed in 1865, abolishes slavery throughout the United States.
- The Fourteenth Amendment, passed in 1868, has four basic provisions:
  1. Defines citizenship and the rights of citizens
  2. Protects voting rights of all citizens or the population basis for representation will be reduced
  3. Bars certain former members of the Confederate government from elected office
  4. Repudiates the public debt obligations of the Confederate government
- Finally, the Fifteenth Amendment, passed in 1870, extends the right to vote to African American men.

PRETEST

Write the provision number in the blank.

5. The Fourteenth Amendment declares the following: "No State shall make or enforce any law which shall abridge the privileges or immunities of citizens of the United States; nor shall any State deprive any person of life, liberty, or property, without due process of law; nor deny to any person within its jurisdiction the equal protection of the laws." Which provision of that amendment does that statement reflect?

___

___

___

6. Which statement *best* explains the sequence of these amendments?

   A. First: slavery abolished; Second: right to vote of former enslaved males guaranteed; Third: citizenship of former enslaved people established
   B. First: right to vote of former enslaved males guaranteed; Second: citizenship of former enslaved people established; Third: slavery abolished
   C. First: citizenship of former enslaved people established; Second: slavery abolished; Third: right to vote of former enslaved males guaranteed
   D. First: slavery abolished; Second: citizenship of former enslaved people established; Third: right to vote of former enslaved males guaranteed

7. Which level of government has the power to create local governments?

   A. county
   B. federal
   C. municipal
   D. state

PRETEST

Question 8 is based on the following graph:

Internal Revenue Service Receipts by Category, 2010 (percentages)

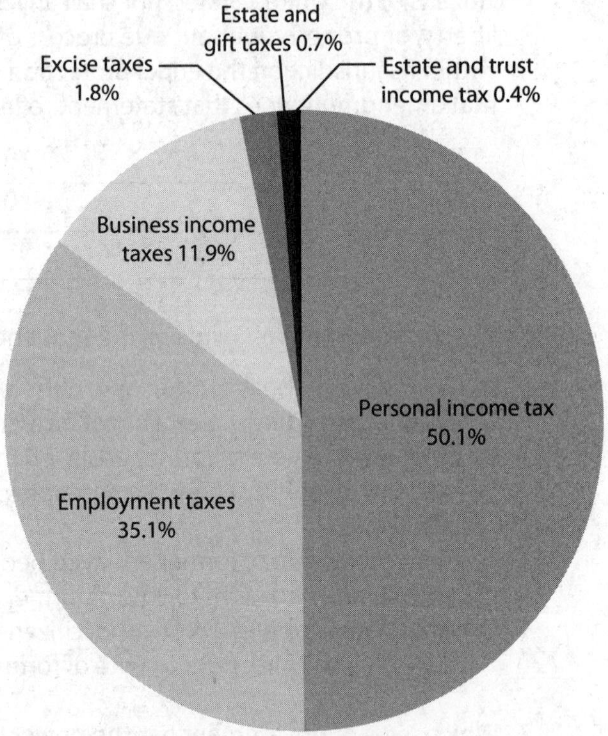

Source: U.S. Bureau of the Census *Statistical Abstract of 2012.*

8. Income taxes paid by individuals account for approximately how much more of Internal Revenue Service receipts than business income taxes?

A. half as much
B. twice as much
C. four times more
D. five times more

PRETEST

The following sentence contains a blank marked Select . . . ▼. *Beneath it is a set of choices. Indicate the choice that is correct and belongs in the blank. (**Note**: On the real GED® test, the choices will appear as a "drop-down" menu. When you click on a choice, it will appear in the blank.)*

9. The law of supply and demand states that as the price for a product increases, the supply of that product__________.

Select . . . ▼
increases
decreases

Questions 10–11 are based on the following chart:

Economic Systems

System	Characteristic	Benefits and Drawbacks
Traditional	Answers basic economic questions by following past patterns	Little freedom of choice Meets basic needs of society, but for limited population Uses resources fairly efficiently Low productivity Little innovation Little variety of goods and services
Market	Individuals and businesses answer the basic economic questions by acting on self-interest	High freedom of choice Opportunity of reward, but with risk High productivity High innovation Great variety of goods and services High-quality goods and services Little protection from market failures, such as monopoly, unfair practices, pollution, business cycle
Command	Government answers the basic economic questions	Low freedom of choice Low productivity Low innovation Relatively low variety of goods and services Relatively low quality of goods and services High level of security through guaranteed employment, social services
Mixed	Individuals answer the basic economic questions by acting on self-interest, but government plays a role to address market failures	Benefits of market economy but at slightly reduced levels (e.g., less freedom of choice) Reduced risks of market economy Cost of government

PRETEST

10. Based on the information in the chart, which type of economy is most likely the second most productive?

    A. command
    B. market
    C. mixed
    D. traditional

11. Which aspect of the U.S. economy reflects its roots in a capitalist, or market, economic system?

    A. opportunities given entrepreneurs
    B. product safety laws
    C. regulation of monopolies
    D. the Social Security system

12. Which of the following illustrates a complementary good for dry cleaning, such that a decrease in the price of the good would cause increased demand for that service?

    A. wool suits
    B. T-shirts
    C. jeans
    D. cotton socks

PRETEST

Questions 13–14 are based on the following graph:

Urban-Rural Population of the United States, 1900–2010

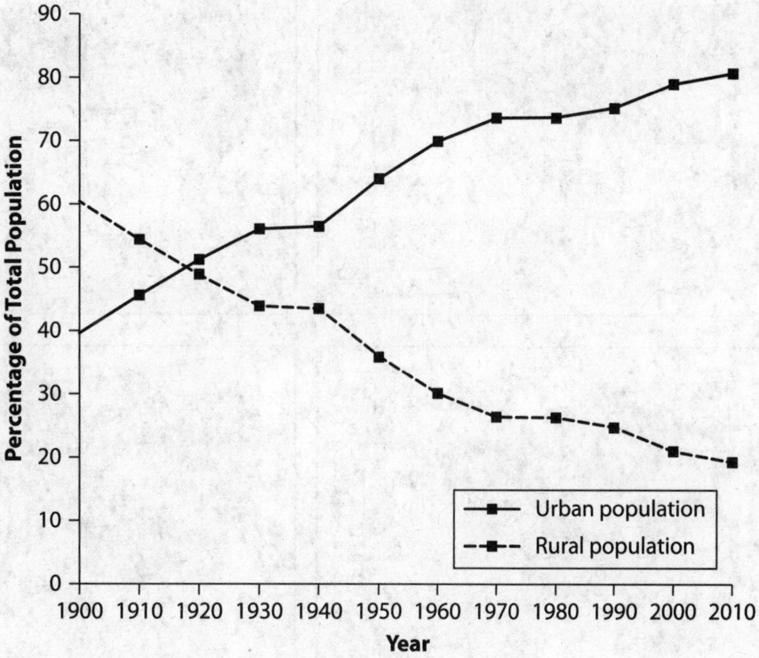

Source: U.S. Bureau of the Census.

13. How much did the U.S. urban population change from 1950 to 2010?
    A. It approximately doubled.
    B. It decreased by almost half.
    C. It decreased to about a third.
    D. It increased about 15 percentage points.

14. Which decade saw no growth in urbanization?
    A. 1900s
    B. 1930s
    C. 2000s
    D. 2010s

PRETEST

Questions 15–17 are based on the following maps:

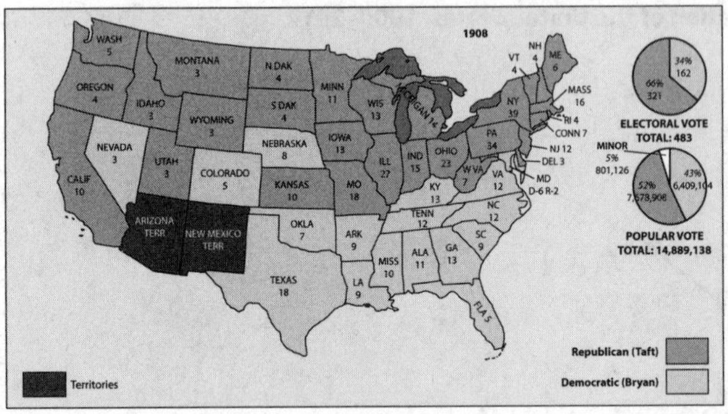

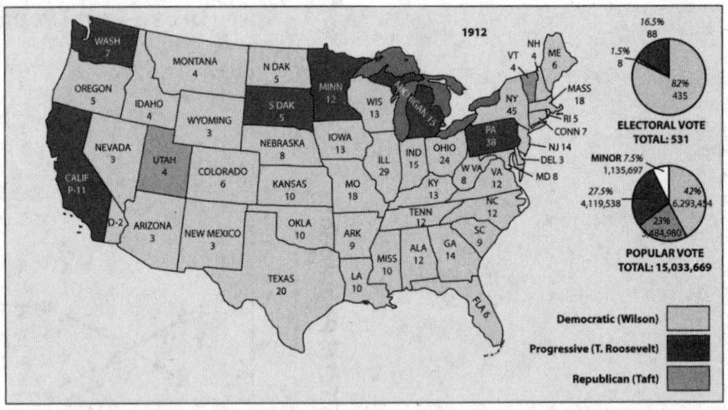

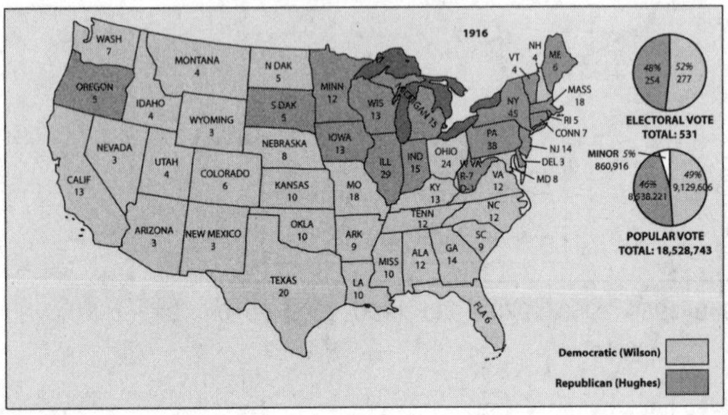

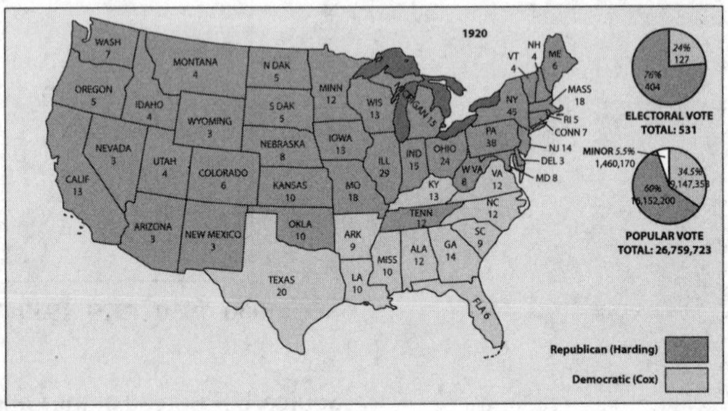

Write the election year in the blank.

15. The election of ______________ shows the best result for a third-party candidate of the four elections.

16. Which statement explains why Arizona and New Mexico are not included in the election results in 1908?

    A. They were territories and thus did not have eligible voters.
    B. Their votes were counted too late to be in the final total.
    C. They were still part of Mexico.
    D. Their votes were counted with California's.

PRETEST

17. Put these elections in order from the closest margin in the electoral college to the widest margin in the electoral college.

*Write the correct year in each box. (**Note**: On the real GED® test, you will click on the items and "drag" each one into the correct box.)*

Electoral College Result	Election Year
closest margin	
↓	
↓	
widest margin	

1908
1912
1916
1920

Questions 18–19 are based on the following quotation:

"If we apply the principle for which the State of Maryland contends, to the constitution generally, we shall find it capable of changing totally the character of that instrument. We shall find it capable of arresting all the measures of the government, and of prostrating it at the foot of the States. The American people have declared their constitution, and the laws made in pursuance thereof, to be supreme; but this principle would transfer the supremacy, in fact, to the States.

If the States may tax one instrument, employed by the government in the execution of its powers, they may tax any and every other instrument. . . . This was not intended by the American people. They did not design to make their government dependent on the States. . . .

. . . The States have no power, by taxation or otherwise, to retard, impede, burden, or in any manner control, the operations of the constitutional laws enacted by Congress to carry into execution the powers vested in the general government. This is, we think, the unavoidable consequence of that supremacy which the constitution has declared.

We are unanimously of opinion, that the law passed by the legislature of Maryland, imposing a tax on the Bank of the United States, is unconstitutional and void."

—Chief Justice John Marshall,
McCullough v. Maryland (1819)

PRETEST

18. In this decision, Chief Justice John Marshall set what precedent?
    A. declaring a law passed by Congress to be unconstitutional
    B. declaring a state law to be unconstitutional
    C. declaring an action taken by the president to be unconstitutional
    D. overturning an earlier Supreme Court decision

19. On which part of the U.S. Constitution did Marshall base his decision?
    A. the commerce clause
    B. due process protections
    C. the judicial review clause
    D. the supremacy clause

Questions 20–21 are based on the following graphs:

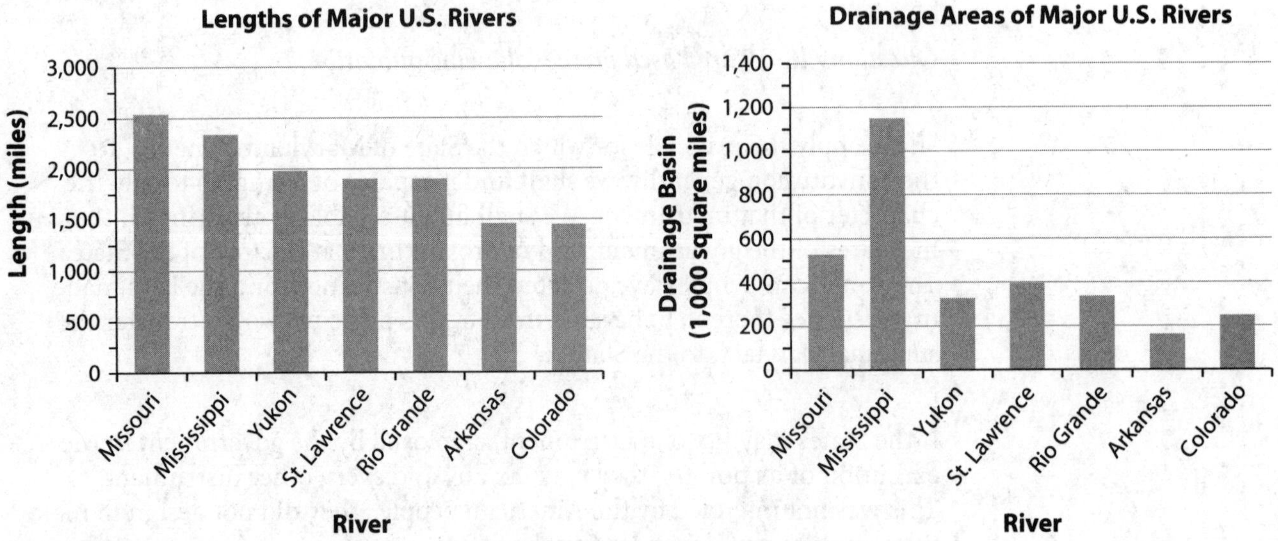

Source: U.S. Bureau of the Census *Statistical Abstract of 2012.*

20. Which is the longest river in the United States, and which has the largest drainage basin?
    A. Missouri; Mississippi
    B. Mississippi; Missouri
    C. Yukon; Mississippi
    D. St. Lawrence; Rio Grande

21. Which statement *best* explains why rivers that are longer than other rivers nevertheless may have smaller drainage basins?
    A. Drainage decreases as length increases.
    B. The shorter the river, the wider and larger the drainage basin.
    C. Drainage depends on how many tributaries a river has.
    D. Drainage basin size has no relation to a river's length.

PRETEST

Questions 22–24 are based on the following map:

Territorial Expansion of the United States

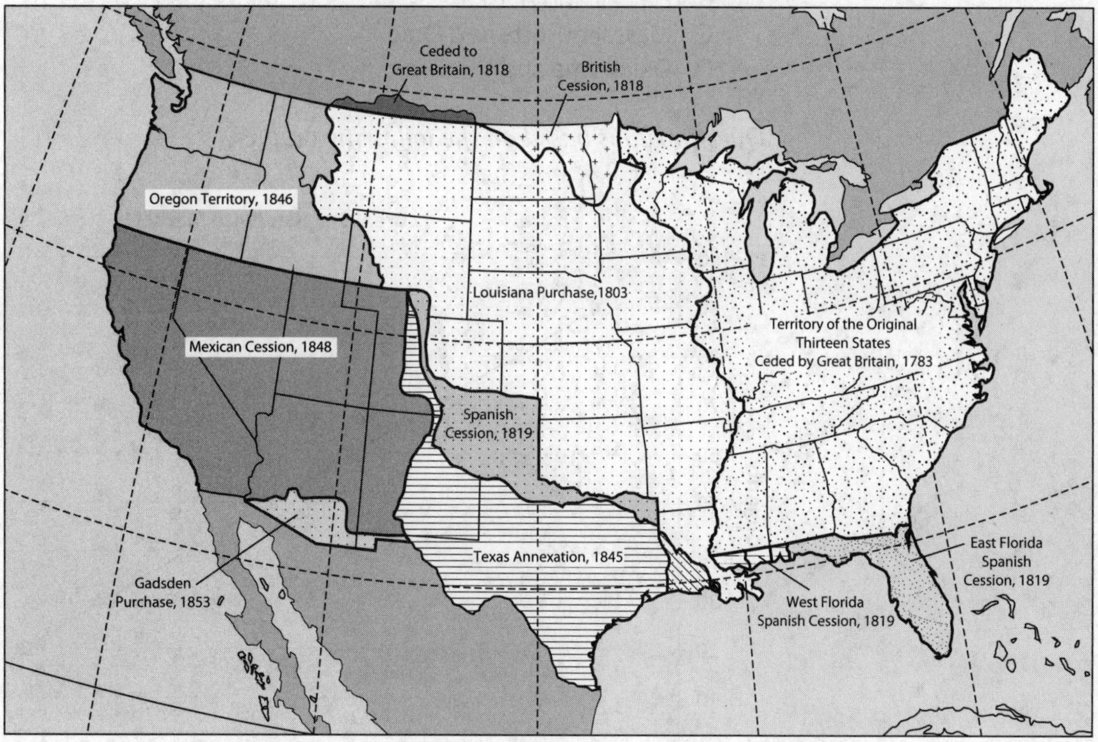

22. How and when did the United States gain what is now Florida?

    A. from Britain in 1783
    B. from Spain in 1819
    C. in the Louisiana Purchase in 1803
    D. from Mexico in 1848

23. Put these four states in the order in which they were acquired.

*Write the correct state in each box. (**Note**: On the real GED® test, you will click on the items and "drag" each one into the correct box.)*

Order Acquired	State
1st	
2nd	
3rd	
4th	

Florida
California
Pennsylvania
Missouri

PRETEST

24. Which states that are now part of the United States do not appear on this map?

A. Georgia and Alabama
B. Hawaii and Alaska
C. Massachusetts and Ohio
D. Oklahoma and Virginia

Question 25 is based on the following graph:

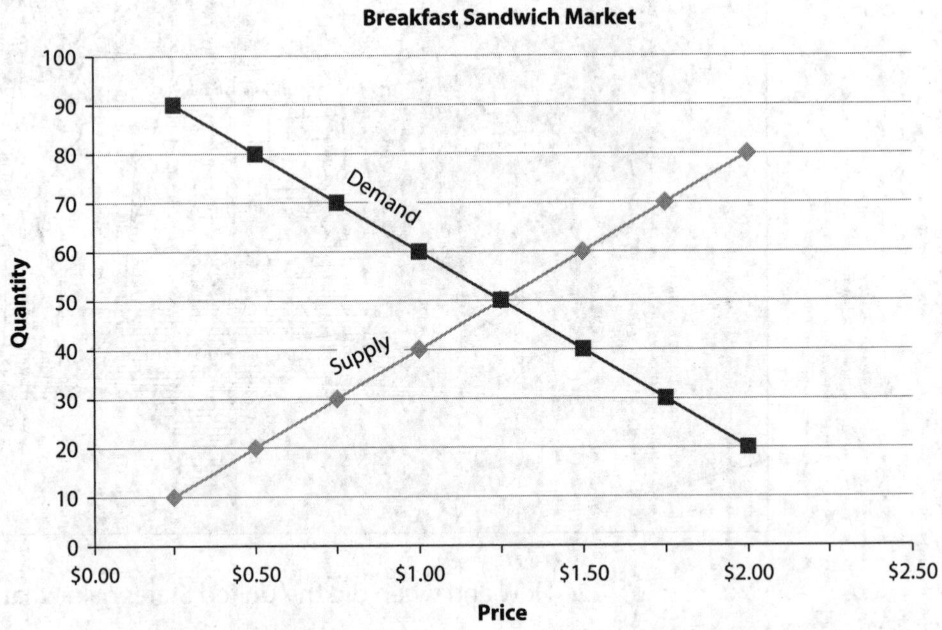

25. Indicate the point on the graph where the price for breakfast sandwiches in this market reaches equilibrium. (***Note****: On the real GED® test, you will click on the spot on the graph you want to select.*)

26. Social Security taxes paid by workers and employers would be part of which category of taxes?

A. business income taxes
B. employment taxes
C. excise taxes
D. personal income taxes

PRETEST

Questions 27–29 are based on the following graph:

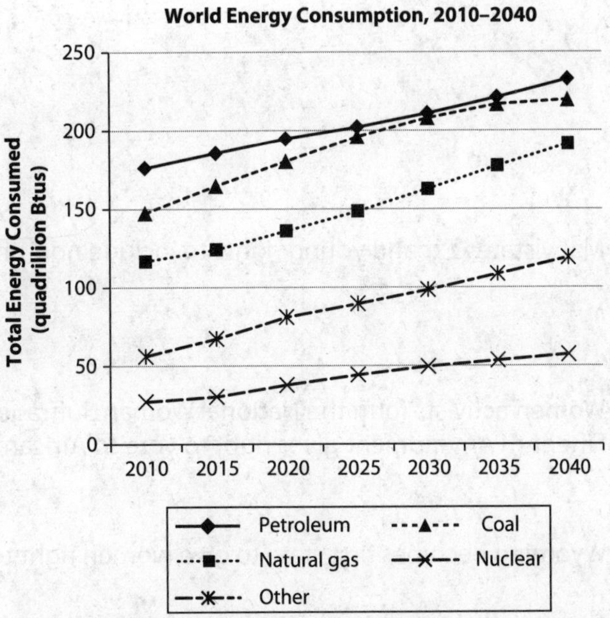

Source: U.S. Energy Information Administration, *International Energy Outlook 2013.*

27. What is expected to be the leading source of energy in the world in 2040?

    A. coal
    B. petroleum
    C. natural gas
    D. nuclear

28. Which category would include hydroelectric power and other renewable sources of energy?

    A. coal
    B. petroleum
    C. natural gas
    D. other

29. Consumption of which energy source is expected to grow most rapidly over the period shown on the graph?

    A. petroleum
    B. natural gas
    C. nuclear
    D. other

PRETEST

Questions 30–32 are based on the following timeline:

1830s	Many states expand voting rights to include non-property-owning white males
1869	Women activists form the National Woman Suffrage Association
1870	Fifteenth Amendment gives right to vote to African American males
1890	Wyoming becomes first state to give women right to vote
1920	Nineteenth Amendment giving women the right to vote is ratified
1924	Congress passes law recognizing Native Americans as citizens and thus giving them the right to vote (although some states banned them from voting)
1943	The Chinese Exclusion Act is repealed; Chinese persons are permitted to become citizens
1952	Under the McCarran-Walter Act, first-generation Japanese Americans are permitted to become citizens
1964	Twenty-First Amendment, outlawing poll tax, is ratified
1965	Congress passes Voting Rights Act to enforce voting rights for African Americans and Native Americans
1971	Twenty-Sixth Amendment, lowering voting age from 21 to 18, is ratified

(Timeline scale: 1776, 1800, 1850, 1900, 1950, 2000)

30. Which action regarding voting happened as a result of the civil rights movement?

    A. ratification of the Fifteenth Amendment
    B. ratification of the Nineteenth Amendment
    C. formation of the National Woman Suffrage Association
    D. passage of the Voting Rights Act

31. Which group received voting rights most recently?

    A. African American males
    B. 18- to 21-year-olds
    C. Native Americans
    D. women

PRETEST

32. Which of the following shows the correct order in which the groups received voting rights?

 A. women, African American males, 18- to 21-year-olds
 B. Native Americans, African American males, 18- to 21-year-olds
 C. white men without property, women, Native Americans
 D. women, African American males, Native Americans

33. President Abraham Lincoln had issued the Emancipation Proclamation during the Civil War. Why, then, was the Thirteenth Amendment necessary?

 A. The Supreme Court had ruled the Emancipation Proclamation unconstitutional.
 B. The Emancipation Proclamation had applied only to parts of the South.
 C. The Emancipation Proclamation had only been a temporary measure.
 D. State governments had not enforced the provisions of the Emancipation Proclamation.

Question 34 is based on the following passage:

Changes in market conditions often have effects on both the supply and demand of a product. If new technology cuts production costs for a product, the supply of that product will increase. If a substitute for a certain product is introduced to the market, the supply of the original product will decrease along with the demand for that original product. If the price of a complementary product falls, then the demand for the main product will increase along with the demand for the complementary product. When government regulation of a product increases, the supply of the product will decrease. When unemployment rises, supply and demand both decrease. However, when prices are expected to rise in the future, supply decreases but demand will increase.

34. While demand generally increases if consumers expect a rise in prices in the future, to which of the following goods is that dynamic *least* likely to apply?

 A. cars
 B. computers
 C. fresh food
 D. stock shares

35. After the end of the Cold War, the former communist states of Eastern Europe and Russia made what economic shift?

 A. from traditional to mixed economies
 B. from command to mixed economies
 C. from mixed to marked economies
 D. from market to command economies

PRETEST

Question 36 is based on the following quotation:

"Every Bill which shall have passed the House of Representatives and the Senate, shall, before it become a Law, be presented to the President of the United States; If he approve he shall sign it, but if not he shall return it, with his Objections to that House in which it shall have originated, who shall enter the Objections at large on their Journal, and proceed to reconsider it. If after such Reconsideration two thirds of that House shall agree to pass the Bill, it shall be sent, together with the Objections, to the other House, by which it shall likewise be reconsidered, and if approved by two thirds of that House, it shall become a Law. But in all such Cases the Votes of both Houses shall be determined by yeas and Nays, and the Names of the Persons voting for and against the Bill shall be entered on the Journal of each House respectively."

—U.S. Constitution, Article I, Section 7

36. What process does this passage describe?
   - A. confirmation of presidential appointments
   - B. impeachment
   - C. naturalization
   - D. veto and override

Question 37 is based on the following quotation:

"It will be our wish and purpose that the processes of peace, when they are begun, shall be absolutely open and that they shall involve and permit henceforth no secret understandings of any kind. The day of conquest and aggrandizement is gone by; so is also the day of secret covenants entered into in the interest of particular governments and likely at some unlooked-for moment to upset the peace of the world. . . .

We entered this war because violations of right had occurred which touched us to the quick and made the life of our own people impossible unless they were corrected and the world secure once for all against their recurrence. What we demand in this war, therefore, is nothing peculiar to ourselves. It is that the world be made fit and safe to live in; and particularly that it be made safe for every peace-loving nation which, like our own, wishes to live its own life, determine its own institutions, be assured of justice and fair dealing by the other peoples of the world as against force and selfish aggression. All the peoples of the world are in effect partners in this interest, and for our own part we see very clearly that unless justice be done to others it will not be done to us. The programme of the world's peace, therefore, is our programme; and that programme, the only possible programme."

—President Woodrow Wilson,
speech to Congress

37. The points that President Wilson detailed in his speech were meant to structure the peace settlement ending what conflict?

A. the American Revolution
B. the Civil War
C. World War I
D. World War II

Questions 38–40 are based on the following passage:

The Bill of Rights is the first ten Amendments to the Constitution. It spells out Americans' rights in relation to their government. It guarantees civil rights and liberties to the individual—like freedom of speech, press, and religion. It sets rules for due process of law and reserves all powers not delegated to the Federal Government to the people or the States. And it specifies that "the enumeration in the Constitution, of certain rights, shall not be construed to deny or disparage others retained by the people."

The First Amendment provides several rights protections: to express ideas through speech and the press, to assemble or gather with a group to protest or for other reasons, and to ask the government to fix problems. It also protects the right to religious beliefs and practices. It prevents the government from creating or favoring a religion.

The Second Amendment protects the right to keep and bear arms.

The Third Amendment prevents government from forcing homeowners to allow soldiers to use their homes. Before the Revolutionary War, laws gave British soldiers the right to take over private homes.

The Fourth Amendment bars the government from unreasonable search and seizure of an individual or their private property.

The Fifth Amendment provides several protections for people accused of crimes. It states that serious criminal charges must be started by a grand jury. A person cannot be tried twice for the same offense (double jeopardy) or have property taken away without just compensation. People have the right against self-incrimination and cannot be imprisoned without due process of law (fair procedures and trials).

The Sixth Amendment provides additional protections to people accused of crimes, such as the right to a speedy and public trial, trial by an impartial jury in criminal cases, and to be informed of criminal charges. Witnesses must face the accused, and the accused is allowed his or her own witnesses and to be represented by a lawyer.

PRETEST

The Seventh Amendment extends the right to a jury trial in Federal civil cases.

The Eighth Amendment bars excessive bail and fines and cruel and unusual punishment.

The Ninth Amendment states that listing specific rights in the Constitution does not mean that people do not have other rights that have not been spelled out.

The Tenth Amendment says that the Federal Government only has those powers delegated in the Constitution. If it isn't listed, it belongs to the states or to the people.

Source: Excerpted from archives.gov

[Source: https://www.archives.gov/founding-docs/bill-of-rights/what-does-it-say#:~:text=The%20Bill%20of%20Rights%20is,speech%2C%20press%2C%20and%20religion.]

38. Which amendment in the Bill of Rights is the basis of the claim of some legal thinkers that capital punishment is unconstitutional?

    A. First
    B. Fifth
    C. Sixth
    D. Eighth

39. When police have a person in custody whom they wish to question regarding possible involvement in a crime, they are required, as a result of the Supreme Court decision in *Miranda v. Arizona*, to read this statement:

    "You have the right to remain silent. Anything you say can and will be used against you in a court of law. You have a right to an attorney. If you cannot afford an attorney, one will be appointed for you."

    Based on the passage, this statement is meant to protect the accused person's rights under which amendments of the Bill of Rights?

    A. First and Second
    B. Third and Fourth
    C. Fifth and Sixth
    D. Seventh and Eighth

PRETEST

Question 40 is based on the following quote from the Ninth Amendment.

"The enumeration in the Constitution, of certain rights, shall not be construed to deny or disparage others retained by the people."

40. What does the word *enumeration* mean?
    - A. mentioning several things one by one
    - B. counting how many times something appears
    - C. explaining the meaning of something
    - D. listing things in the order of their importance

THIS IS THE END OF THE SOCIAL STUDIES PRETEST.

PRETEST

Answers and Explanations

1. **popular sovereignty** "We the people . . . do ordain and establish" means that the people have the power. This is popular sovereignty.

2. **A** The president makes treaties, but the Senate must approve. This is our system of checks and balances.

3. **B** The amendments in the Bill of Rights establish the rights of the people and limit the powers of the federal government.

4. **A** When production costs are lower, profits are higher. Suppliers increase supply to gain more of those higher profits.

5. **1** The quote relates to the rights of citizens, which is the first provision.

6. **D** In 1865 slavery is abolished; in 1868 citizenship is granted to former slaves; in 1870 African American men are given the right to vote.

7. **C** Local governments are established by municipal governments.

8. **C** Individual taxes account for 50.1% and business income taxes account for 11.9%. $50.1 \div 11.9 = 4.21$. This is approximately four times more.

9. **increases** The law of supply states that as price increases, supply increases.

10. **C** The chart states that market economies are highly productive and that mixed economies have the same benefits, though slightly reduced. Therefore, mixed economy is likely to be the second most productive.

11. **A** A market economy has high freedom of choice and high innovation. This favors entrepreneurs.

12. **A** If wool suits were cheaper, demand for them would be higher. Because wool suits must be dry cleaned, this would also increase demand for that service.

13. **D** The urban population in 1950 was approximately 63%. In 2010, it was approximately 78%. That is an increase of 15%.

14. **B** Urban growth stayed the same from 1930–1940 and then again from 1970–1980. Only the 1930s is an answer choice.

15. **1912** In 1912, the third-party candidate received electoral votes and a large percentage of the popular vote.

16. **A** According to the map key, Arizona and New Mexico were territories rather than states in 1908.

17.

Electoral College Result	Election Year
closest margin	1916
↓	1908
↓	1920
widest margin	1912

18. **B** The last paragraph says that the state law is unconstitutional.

19. **D** The first and third paragraphs mention the supremacy of the U.S. Constitution.

20. **A** According to the charts, the Missouri River is the longest at 2500 miles, and the Mississippi River has the largest drainage basin at approximately 1.15 million square miles.

21. **C** If a river has many tributaries, it spreads out the drainage, resulting in a larger drainage basin.

PRETEST

22. **B** The map shows that Florida became part of the United States through "Spanish Cession, 1819."

23.

Order Acquired	State
1st	Pennsylvania
2nd	Missouri
3rd	Florida
4th	California

24. **B** The map does not show Alaska or Hawaii.

25. **$1.25** The supply and demand lines meet at $1.25.

26. **B** If the taxes are paid by workers and employers, they are part of employment taxes.

27. **B** The top line on the graph in 2040 is for petroleum.

28. **D** They are not shown on the graph, so would be included in the category for "other."

29. **B** The steepest increase is for the natural gas line.

30. **D** The Voting Rights Act was passed in 1965 during the civil rights movement.

31. **B** The Twenty-Sixth Amendment in 1971 gave 18-year-olds the right to vote.

32. **C** White men who did not own property got the vote in the 1830s; women got the vote in 1920; Native Americans got the vote in 1924.

33. **B** The Thirteenth Amendment abolished slavery in all states. The Emancipation Proclamation only abolished slavery in the rebelling Confederate states.

34. **C** The demand for fresh foods would not increase because of an expected future price increase, as fresh food must be used very soon after purchase.

35. **B** Communist countries have command economies. After the Cold War, many shifted to mixed economies.

36. **D** The passage discusses how a president may veto a bill and how Congress can override the veto.

37. **C** President Wilson served during World War I.

38. **D** The objection that some make to capital punishment is that it violates the Eighth Amendment ban on cruel and unusual punishment.

39. **C** The Miranda warning is a reminder of the Fifth Amendment right not to testify against oneself and the Sixth Amendment right to legal counsel.

40. **A** *Enumeration* here means listing each right one by one. The Ninth Amendment says that even though a right may not be specifically listed in the Constitution, it remains with the people.

PRETEST

Evaluation Chart

Circle the number of each question that you missed. To the right of the numbers below, you will find the titles of the chapters that cover the skills you need to solve the problems. More question numbers circled in any row means more attention is needed to sharpen those skills for the GED® Test.

Question Numbers	Chapter
1, 2, 3, 7, 8, 15, 16, 17, 18, 19, 26, 36, 38, 39	Civics and Government
2, 5, 6, 20, 22, 23, 30, 31, 32, 33, 37	U.S. History
4, 9, 10, 11, 12, 25, 34, 35	Economics
13, 14, 20, 21, 24, 27, 28, 29	Geography and the World

If you find you need instruction before you are ready to practice with this workbook, we offer several excellent options:

McGraw-Hill Education Preparation for the GED® Test: This book contains a complete test preparation program with intensive review and practice for the topics tested on the GED®.

McGraw-Hill Education Pre-GED®: This book is a beginner's guide for students who need to develop a solid foundation or refresh basic skills before they embark on formal preparation for the GED® test.

McGraw-Hill Education Short Course for the GED®: This book provides a concise review of all the essential topics on the GED®, with numerous additional practice questions.

CHAPTER 1

Civics and Government

Directions: Answer the following questions. For multiple-choice questions, choose the best answer. For other questions, follow the directions preceding the question. Answers begin on page 171.

Questions 1–2 are based on the following quotation:

"All men are naturally in . . . a state of perfect freedom to order their actions, and dispose of their possessions and persons, as they think fit, within the bounds of the law of nature, without asking leave [of], or depending upon the will of any other man."

—John Locke, *Second Treatise on Government*

1. Which principle that contributed to American constitutional democracy does this quotation represent?

   A. natural rights philosophy
   B. consent of the governed
   C. majority rule
   D. separation of powers

2. Which of the following phrases from the U.S. Declaration of Independence reflects Locke's thinking in this quotation?

   A. "Whenever any Form of Government becomes destructive of these ends, it is the Right of the People to alter or to abolish it."
   B. "We, therefore . . . declare, That these United Colonies are, and of Right ought to be Free and Independent States."
   C. "All men . . . are endowed by their Creator with certain unalienable Rights."
   D. "The history of the present King of Great Britain is a history of repeated injuries and usurpations."

Questions 3–4 are based on the following diagram:

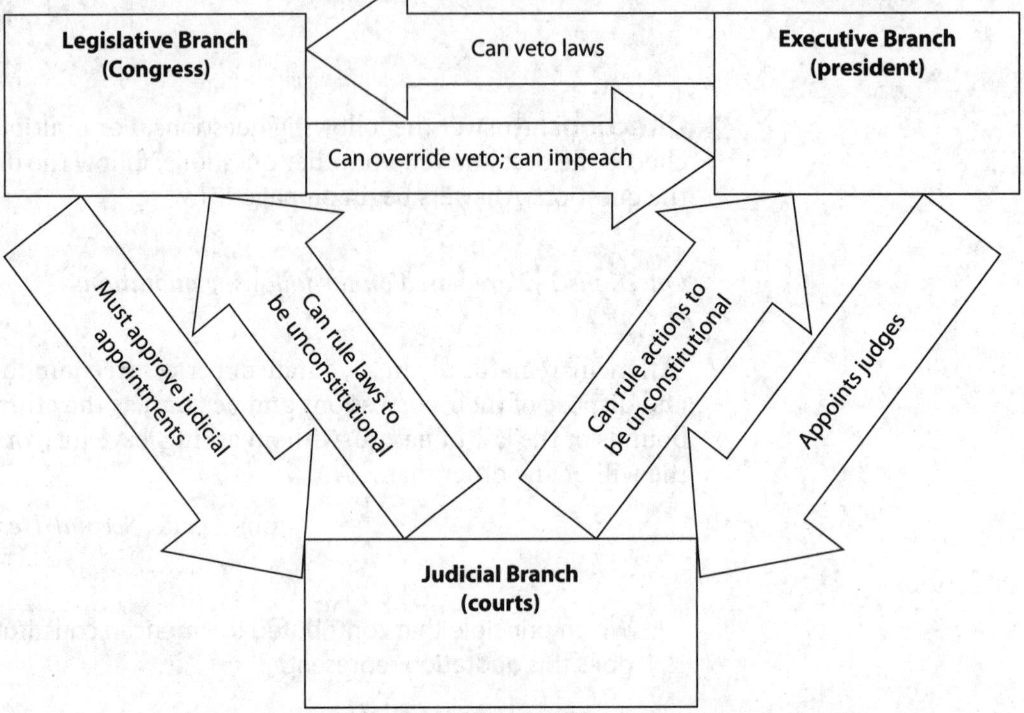

3. *Indicate the box where each of the following items belongs. (**Note:** On the real GED® test, you will click on the items and "drag" each one into the correct box.)*

veto power	impeachment power
declaring acts unconstitutional	appointment power

Checks by President on Other Branches	
Checks on Presidential Power	

4. What was the purpose of the delegates at the Constitutional Convention in creating the system of checks and balances?

   A. to ensure popular sovereignty
   B. to limit government power
   C. to promote the federal system
   D. to guarantee majority rule

5. What is the form of government of the United States and each of the fifty states?

   A. representative democracy
   B. direct democracy
   C. parliamentary democracy
   D. presidential democracy

6. Which of the following is a modern example of direct democracy?

   A. Athenian democracy
   B. state legislatures
   C. school boards
   D. New England town meetings

Questions 7–9 are based on the following chart:

State Powers	Shared Powers	Federal Powers
• Register voters and carry out elections	• Pass and enforce laws	• Print money
• Form county and city governments	• Create courts	• Maintain an army and navy
• Create and oversee public schools	• Tax individuals and businesses	• Manage relations with other countries, including making treaties and declaring war
• Grant licenses for driving, marriage, and other activities	• Borrow money	• Regulate commerce between states
• Regulate commerce within state	• Build highways and bridges	• Create and run the postal system
• Ratify amendments to the Constitution	• Grant charters to banks, corporations	• Conduct a census every 10 years
		• Grant patents and copyrights

7. Which statement *best* explains why both the state and federal governments have the power to tax?

   A. Politicians generally favor high taxes.
   B. Governments must have revenue to be able to act.
   C. The American system is built on double taxation.
   D. Taxation without representation is tyranny.

Federalism – a mixed or compound mode of government that combines a general government with regional governments in a single political system

8. A trade agreement with Canada would fall under federal authority on the basis of which power?

   A. regulating commerce between states
   B. creating and running the postal system
   C. granting charters to banks
   D. managing relations with other countries

9. Which principle of the U.S. Constitution is demonstrated by the division of powers between the state and federal governments shown in the chart?

   A. federalism
   B. separation of powers
   C. check and balances
   D. popular sovereignty

10. Under the U.S. Constitution, what is the chief responsibility assigned to the vice president of the United States?

    A. attend official meetings on behalf of the president
    B. preside over Senate sessions
    C. cast tie-breaking votes in the House
    D. advise the president

George washington precedent.
FDR
1947 - 22nd amendment
- 2 term limit

Question 11 is based on the following passage:

The United States can be characterized as a Presidential Democracy and Great Britain can be characterized as a Parliamentary Democracy. While both the President of the United States and the Prime Minister of Great Britain head the executive branch of their respective governments, there are some significant differences between them. The British prime minister is elected by voters from one parliamentary district, then chosen by members of Parliament. The U.S. president is elected by all of a country's voters via the electoral college system. The British prime minister serves a maximum term of five years before new elections must be held, but there is no limit on the number of terms that may be served. In contrast, the U.S. president serves a maximum of two four-year terms.

The leaders also differ in terms of the powers they exert over other parts of the government. The U.S. president appoints members of the cabinet, with Senate approval, and can fire people without approval. The British prime minister appoints and fires members of cabinet, although the monarch must approve those decisions. The U.S. president cannot disband Congress and force new elections, but the British prime minister can disband Parliament and force new elections. The U.S. president also has the power to veto bills, while the British prime minister does not have the power to veto bills.

11. What is a major difference between the British prime minister and the U.S. president?

   A. The prime minister, not the president, has the power to disband the legislature and force new elections.
   B. The prime minister, not the president, has the power to veto bills.
   C. The president, not the prime minister, has no term limits.
   D. The president, not the prime minister, is also a member of the legislature.

12. *Indicate the box where each of the following items belongs. (**Note:** On the real GED® test, you will click on the items and "drag" each one into the correct box.)*

president	member of the U.S. House
vice president	U.S. senator

Two-Year Term	
Four-Year Term	
Six-Year Term	

13. *The following sentence contains a blank marked* Select... ▼. *Beneath it is a set of choices. Indicate the choice that is correct and belongs in the blank. (**Note:** On the real GED® test, the choices will appear as a "drop-down" menu. When you click on a choice, it will appear in the blank.)*

The president is elected by a majority of Select... ▼ .

Select... ▼
popular votes
members of each house of Congress
electoral votes

14. Which official serves for life, unless removed from office by impeachment?

A. member of the U.S. House
B. president
C. Supreme Court justice
D. U.S. senator

Questions 15–16 are based on the following quotation:

"A well regulated Militia, being necessary to the security of a free State, the right of the people to keep and bear Arms, shall not be infringed."

—U.S. Constitution, Second Amendment (ratified 1781)

15. This amendment is at the heart of what contemporary public policy issue?

    A. government intelligence gathering on U.S. citizens
    B. civilian control of the military
    C. gun control
    D. limits on immigration

16. Many opponents of any laws to place limits on gun ownership base their opposition on this amendment. Which of the following is the best legal argument to counter that position?

    A. "The people who wrote the Bill of Rights could not imagine how murderous modern weapons could be."
    B. "The right to own guns was important when the country had no standing army and a militia was needed for defense."
    C. "The United States has more handgun deaths than any other industrialized country in the world."
    D. "The presence of handguns in a home raises the risk that a child will take the weapon, leading to a tragic accident."

17. The separation of church and state, established by the First Amendment, is used by judges to prohibit which of the following actions?

    A. abortion
    B. stem-cell research
    C. gay marriage
    D. prayer in public school

18. In 1992, the U.S. Supreme Court ruled (in *R.A.V. v. City of St. Paul*) that a Minnesota law that made it illegal to burn a cross for the purpose of arousing anger or resentment against an individual or group on the basis of that individual's or group's race, color, religion, or gender would be overturned. What was *most likely* the rationale for the Court's decision to overturn this law?

    A. The law violated the First Amendment right of free speech.
    B. The law violated the Fifth Amendment protection of due process.
    C. The law violated the Eighth Amendment ban on cruel and unusual punishment.
    D. The law violated the Fourteenth Amendment ban on equal protection under the law.

19. Which of the following individuals would be *most likely* to favor limits on free speech?

    A. an artist whose work challenges traditional religion
    B. a comedian who writes satires about government officials
    C. a researcher who thinks that pornography is linked to violence against children
    D. an antiabortion activist who pickets abortion clinics

Questions 20–23 are based on the following graphs:

Number of Presidential Vetoes

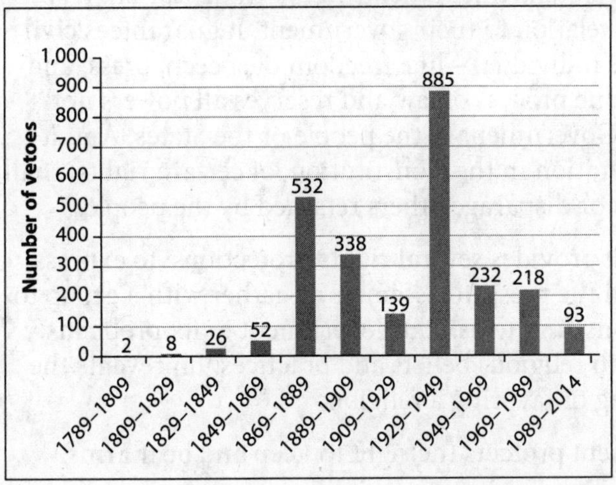

Number of Vetoes Overridden

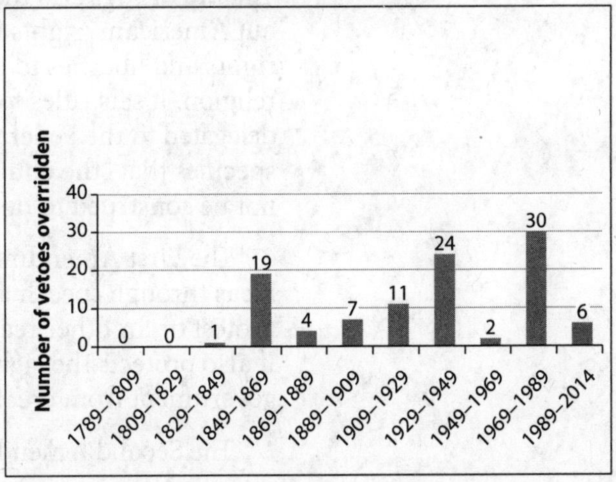

20. Which period saw the most presidential vetoes?

    A. 1869–1889
    B. 1889–1909
    C. 1929–1949
    D. 1969–1989

21. Which generalization can reasonably be made based on the data in the graph of presidential vetoes?

    A. Vetoes were rare until the second half of the nineteenth century.
    B. Vetoes have steadily increased over time.
    C. Vetoes were more frequent in the early years of the United States.
    D. Presidents veto only a fraction of the bills passed by Congress.

22. Which generalization can reasonably be made based on the data in *both* graphs?

    A. Veto overrides have been more common since the mid-1900s.
    B. Overridden vetoes are high when the president and the majority in Congress are from different parties.
    C. Congress succeeds in overriding presidential vetoes relatively infrequently.
    D. The failure of Congress to override vetoes shows that presidents have too much power.

23. Which statement *best* explains why the data about presidential vetoes and overridden vetoes are shown on two graphs?

    A. The two subjects are unrelated.
    B. The magnitude of the data is widely different.
    C. The two sets of years would not fit on one graph.
    D. The two graphs show different kinds of data (numbers and percentages).

Questions 24–27 are based on the following passage:

The Bill of Rights is the first ten Amendments to the Constitution. It spells out Americans' rights in relation to their government. It guarantees civil rights and liberties to the individual—like freedom of speech, press, and religion. It sets rules for due process of law and reserves all powers not delegated to the Federal Government to the people or the States. And it specifies that "the enumeration in the Constitution, of certain rights, shall not be construed to deny or disparage others retained by the people."

The First Amendment provides several rights protections: to express ideas through speech and the press, to assemble or gather with a group to protest or for other reasons, and to ask the government to fix problems. It also protects the right to religious beliefs and practices. It prevents the government from creating or favoring a religion.

The Second Amendment protects the right to keep and bear arms.

The Third Amendment prevents government from forcing homeowners to allow soldiers to use their homes. Before the Revolutionary War, laws gave British soldiers the right to take over private homes.

The Fourth Amendment bars the government from unreasonable search and seizure of an individual or their private property.

The Fifth Amendment provides several protections for people accused of crimes. It states that serious criminal charges must be started by a grand jury. A person cannot be tried twice for the same offense (double jeopardy) or have property taken away without just compensation. People have the right against self-incrimination and cannot be imprisoned without due process of law (fair procedures and trials).

The Sixth Amendment provides additional protections to people accused of crimes, such as the right to a speedy and public trial, trial by an impartial jury in criminal cases, and to be informed of criminal charges. Witnesses must face the accused, and the accused is allowed his or her own witnesses and to be represented by a lawyer.

The Seventh Amendment extends the right to a jury trial in Federal civil cases.

The Eighth Amendment bars excessive bail and fines and cruel and unusual punishment.

The Ninth Amendment states that listing specific rights in the Constitution does not mean that people do not have other rights that have not been spelled out.

The Tenth Amendment says that the Federal Government only has those powers delegated in the Constitution. If it isn't listed, it belongs to the states or to the people.

Source: Excerpted from archives.gov

[Source: https://www.archives.gov/founding-docs/bill-of-rights/what-does-it-say#:~:text=The%20Bill%20of%20Rights%20is,speech%2C%20press%2C%20and%20religion.]

24. *Indicate the box where each of the following items belongs. (**Note:** On the real GED® test, you will click on the items and "drag" each one into the correct box.)*

First	Second	Fourth	Fifth
Sixth	Eighth	Ninth	

Basic Rights	
Rights of the Accused	

25. Based on the description in the passage, which amendment contains the following text?

"... no Warrants shall issue, but upon probable cause, supported by Oath or affirmation, and particularly describing the place to be searched, and the persons or things to be seized ..."

—U.S. Constitution

A. Fourth
B. Fifth
C. Sixth
D. Ninth

26. In 1962, in *Gideon v. Wainwright*, the U.S. Supreme Court ruled that the constitutional right to be represented by a lawyer extended to trials in state court. On which amendment would the Court base that right?

A. First
B. Fourth
C. Fifth
D. Sixth

27. In 2014, in *Riley v. California*, the U.S. Supreme Court ruled unanimously that police could not conduct searches of the contents of an individual's cell phone without a warrant. That ruling was based on the rights protected under which amendment?

A. Third
B. Fourth
C. Fifth
D. Seventh

Questions 28–31 are based on the following texts:

"All persons born or naturalized in the United States, and subject to the jurisdiction thereof, are citizens of the United States and of the State wherein they reside. No State shall make or enforce any law which shall abridge the privileges or immunities of citizens of the United States; nor shall any State deprive any person of life, liberty, or property, without due process of law; nor deny to any person within its jurisdiction the equal protection of the laws."

—U.S. Constitution, Fourteenth Amendment

"The right of citizens of the United States to vote shall not be denied or abridged by the United States or by any State on account of race, color, or previous condition of servitude."

—U.S. Constitution, Fifteenth Amendment

"The right of citizens of the United States to vote shall not be denied or abridged by the United States or by any State on account of sex."

—U.S. Constitution, Nineteenth Amendment

"The right of citizens of the United States to vote in any primary or other election for President or Vice President, for electors for President or Vice President, or for Senator or Representative in Congress, shall not be denied or abridged by the United States or any State by reason of failure to pay any poll tax or other tax."

—U.S. Constitution, Twenty-Fourth Amendment

"The right of citizens of the United States, who are eighteen years of age or older, to vote shall not be denied or abridged by the United States or by any State on account of age."

—U.S. Constitution, Twenty-Sixth Amendment

28. Amendments to the U.S. Constitution are numbered in chronological order. Based on this information, which statement is true?

    A. Eighteen-year-olds got the right to vote before African American men.
    B. Women received the right to vote last of all the groups covered in these amendments.
    C. African American men were declared citizens before they were guaranteed the right to vote.
    D. Outlawing of poll taxes gave women the right to vote.

29. During the Vietnam War in the 1960s and early 1970s, many Americans protested the fact that young men were drafted into the army to serve in the war but did not have the right to vote for the leaders making the decisions about that war. Which amendment was written and ratified in response to those protests?

    A. Fifteenth
    B. Nineteenth
    C. Twenty-Fourth
    D. Twenty-Sixth

30. The poll tax had been enacted in some southern states to suppress voting by poor African Americans. Which statement *best* explains why the Twenty-Fourth Amendment banned the imposition of this tax in elections for president, vice president, and the U.S. Congress only?

    A. These are the most important elections.
    B. State and local election rules are set by the states.
    C. Congress has no interest in state and local elections.
    D. The poll tax was used only in these elections.

31. Which of these voting rights amendments affected the largest share of Americans?

    A. Fifteenth
    B. Nineteenth
    C. Twenty-Fourth
    D. Twenty-Sixth

32. *The following sentence contains a blank marked* Select... ▼. *Beneath it is a set of choices. Indicate the choice that is correct and belongs in the blank. (**Note:** On the real GED® test, the choices will appear as a "drop-down" menu. When you click on a choice, it will appear in the blank.)*

    The Select... ▼ presides over meetings of the House of Representatives.

Select... ▼
Speaker of the House
majority leader
vice president

33. The power of the U.S. Congress to impeach the president, vice president, and federal justices for "high crimes and misdemeanors" is an example of what constitutional principle?

    A. federalism
    B. popular sovereignty
    C. majority rule
    D. rule of law

34. Which of these actions by Congress requires a "supermajority"—approval by two-thirds of all members voting rather than a simple majority of half plus one?

A. passage of a bill
B. approval of a cabinet appointment
C. override of a veto
D. ratification of a treaty

35. *The following sentence contains a blank marked* Select... ▼ *. Beneath it is a set of choices. Indicate the choice that is correct and belongs in the blank. (**Note:** On the real GED® test, the choices will appear as a "drop-down" menu. When you click on a choice, it will appear in the blank.)*

Cabinet departments such as the Department of Defense and Department of Justice belong to the Select... ▼ branch.

Select... ▼
executive
judicial
legislative

36. Which cabinet department includes the Bureau of Land Management, the National Park Service, and the Fish and Wildlife Service?

A. Agriculture
B. Commerce
C. Interior
D. State

Questions 37–38 are based on the following quotation:

"We the People of the United States, in Order to form a more perfect Union, establish Justice, insure domestic Tranquility, provide for the common defence, promote the general Welfare, and secure the Blessings of Liberty to ourselves and our Posterity, do ordain and establish this Constitution for the United States of America."

—U.S. Constitution, Preamble

37. Which constitutional principle is represented in the statement that "We the People . . . ordain and establish" the Constitution?

A. separation of powers
B. federalism
C. popular sovereignty
D. republicanism

38. What is the purpose of the Preamble to the Constitution?

A. to place strict limits on government power
B. to state the goals the Constitution is meant to achieve
C. to clarify the relationship of state and federal power
D. to state the equality of all Americans

Questions 39–40 are based on the following diagram:

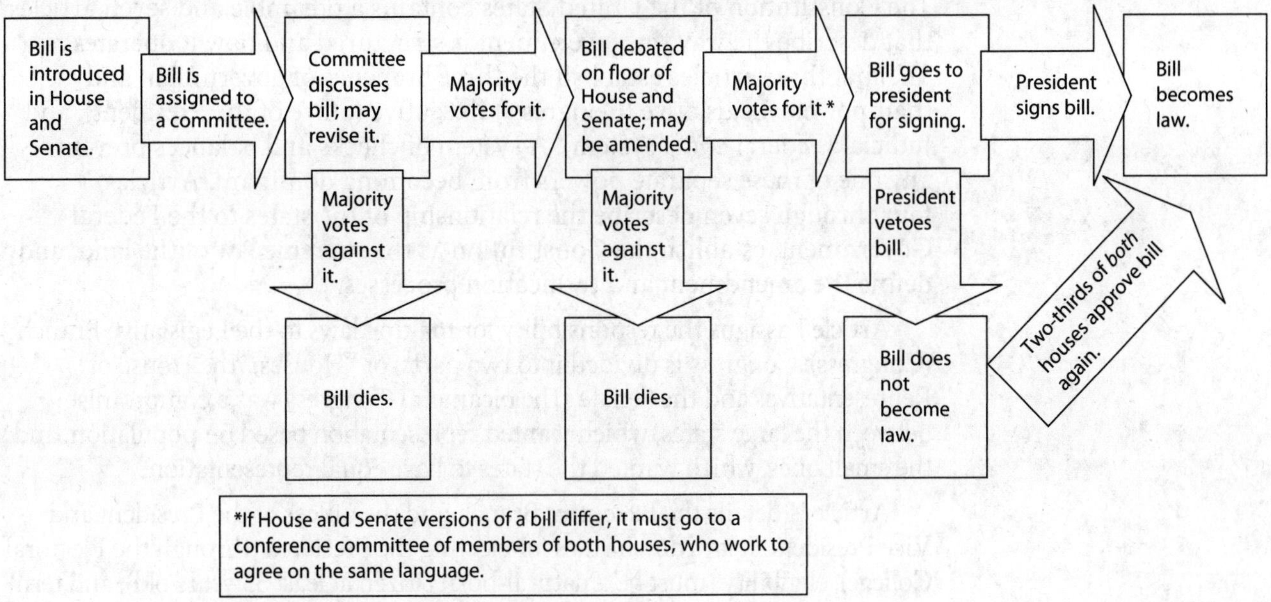

39. Which actions are absolutely essential for a bill to become a law?
    A. approval by committees in both houses and signature by the president
    B. approval by both houses and signature by the president or a vote to override a veto
    C. signature by the president
    D. approval by a conference committee and signature by the president

40. Under what circumstances does a bill go to a conference committee?
    A. If the House and Senate approve different versions of the bill.
    B. If the bill is introduced in both houses.
    C. If the president vetoes the bill.
    D. If both houses vote the bill down.

41. What determines the number of electoral votes a state has?
    A. the number of eligible voters who cast ballots
    B. the number of members in the House and Senate
    C. the number of counties in the state
    D. the number of members in the state legislature

42. In which elections do voters go to the polls to choose candidates for office?
    A. caucus
    B. general
    C. primary
    D. special

Questions 43–44 are based on the following passage:

The Constitution of the United States contains a preamble and seven articles that describe the way the government is structured and how it operates. The first three articles establish the three branches of government and their powers: Legislative (Congress), Executive (office of the President), and Judicial (Federal court system). A system of checks and balances prevents any one of these separate powers from becoming dominant. Articles four through seven describe the relationship of the states to the Federal Government, establish the Constitution as the supreme law of the land, and define the amendment and ratification processes.

Article I assigns the responsibility for making laws to the Legislative Branch (Congress). Congress is divided into two parts, or "Houses," the House of Representatives and the Senate. The bicameral Congress was a compromise between the large states, which wanted representation based on population, and the small ones, which wanted the states to have equal representation.

Article II details the Executive Branch and the offices of the President and Vice President. It lays down rules for electing the President (through the Electoral College), eligibility (must be a natural-born citizen at least 35 years old), and term length. The 12th and 25th Amendments modified some of these rules.

Article III establishes the Judicial Branch with the U.S. Supreme Court as the federal court system's highest court. It specifies that Federal judges be appointed for life unless they commit a serious crime. This article is shorter than Articles I and II. The Federal Convention left much of the work of planning the court system to the First Congress. The 1789 Judiciary Act created the three-tiered court system in place today.

Article IV outlines states' powers in relationship to each other. States have the authority to create and enforce their own laws but must respect and help enforce the laws of other states. Congress may pass Federal laws regarding how states honor other states' laws and records.

Article V explains the amendment process, which is different and more difficult than the process for making laws. When two-thirds of the Senate and two-thirds of the House of Representatives vote to change the Constitution, an amendment goes to the state legislatures for a vote. Alternatively, two-thirds of the state legislatures can submit an application to Congress, and then Congress calls a national convention at which states propose amendments. Three-fourths of the state legislatures or state conventions must vote in favor of an amendment to ratify it.

Article VI states that Federal law is supreme, or higher than, state and local laws. This means that if a state law conflicts with a Federal law, Federal law takes precedence.

Article VII describes the ratification process for the Constitution. It called for special state ratifying conventions. Nine states were required to enact the Constitution. Rhode Island became the 13th state to ratify the Constitution in 1790.

Source: Excerpted from archives.gov

[Source: https://www.archives.gov/founding-docs/constitution/what-does-it-say]

43. Which article of the Constitution authorizes Congress to create federal courts?

    A. Article II
    B. Article III
    C. Article IV
    D. Article V

44. In which article would you find the following quotation?

    "This Constitution, and the Laws of the United States which shall be made in Pursuance thereof; and all Treaties made, or which shall be made, under the Authority of the United States, shall be the supreme Law of the Land; and the Judges in every State shall be bound thereby, any Thing in the Constitution or Laws of any State to the Contrary notwithstanding."

    A. Article IV
    B. Article V
    C. Article VI
    D. Article VII

45. What is one way that interest groups differ from political parties?

    A. Interest groups do not have candidates that run for office.
    B. Interest groups do not influence legislation.
    C. Interest groups do not spend money on political campaigns.
    D. Interest groups focus on specific goals.

46. *The following sentence contains a blank marked* Select . . . ▼ *. Beneath it is a set of choices. Indicate the choice that is correct and belongs in the blank. (**Note:** On the real GED® test, the choices will appear as a "drop-down" menu. When you click on a choice, it will appear in the blank.)*

    On the state level, the office of Select . . . ▼ is comparable to

Select . . . ▼
governor
lieutenant governor
mayor

    the office of president on the national level.

47. Which of the following correctly identifies the interest group and a major issue with which it is involved?

    A. Children's Defense Fund—juvenile justice
    B. Sierra Club—the environment
    C. AARP—health care
    D. Chamber of Commerce—the stock market

Questions 48–50 are based on the following passage from The Federalist Papers:

"From this view of the subject it may be concluded that a pure democracy, by which I mean a society consisting of a small number of citizens, who assemble and administer the government in person, can admit of no cure for the mischiefs of faction. A common passion or interest will, in almost every case, be felt by a majority of the whole; . . . and there is nothing to check the inducements to sacrifice the weaker party or an obnoxious individual. Hence it is that such democracies have ever been spectacles of turbulence and contention; have ever been found incompatible with personal security or the rights of property; and have in general been as short in their lives as they have been violent in their deaths. . . .

A republic, by which I mean a government in which the scheme of representation takes place, opens a different prospect, and promises the cure for which we are seeking. . . .

The two great points of difference between a democracy and a republic are: first, the delegation of the government, in the latter, to a small number of citizens elected by the rest; secondly, the greater number of citizens, and greater sphere of country, over which the latter may be extended."

—James Madison, *The Federalist*, No. 10

48. What defines a republican form of government, according to Madison?
    A. government by consent of the governed
    B. decisions made by elected representatives
    C. decisions made by all citizens as a body
    D. policies favoring low taxes and economic growth

49. What is a disadvantage that "pure democracy" has compared to republican government, according to Madison?
    A. short duration
    B. large extent
    C. lack of competing factions
    D. domination by people of property

50. Why are minority rights at risk in a pure democracy, according to Madison?
    A. Pure democracies are likely to include slavery.
    B. Pure democracies can be easily misled by a tyrannical ruler.
    C. Strong majorities are likely to form and impose their will.
    D. These democracies can only form in societies with shared interests.

Question 51 is based on the following passage from the U.S. Constitution, which defines one of the powers granted to the U.S. Congress:

"[Congress shall have the power] to make all Laws which shall be necessary and proper for carrying into Execution the foregoing Powers, and all other Powers vested by this Constitution in the Government of the United States, or in any Department or Officer thereof."

—U.S. Constitution, Article I, Section 8

51. Why is this "necessary and proper" clause of the U.S. Constitution sometimes called "the elastic clause"?

    A. Congress can stretch it to abuse its power.
    B. The federal government stretches this power to usurp state power.
    C. The president stretches this power in issuing executive orders.
    D. Congress can use the clause to stretch its powers.

52. The Equal Opportunity Employment Commission, which works to prevent and punish discrimination in employment decisions, is an example of federal government efforts to achieve what goal?

    A. promote economic growth
    B. protect minority rights
    C. ensure separation of powers
    D. achieve full employment

53. *The following sentence contains a blank marked* Select... ▼*. Beneath it is a set of choices. Indicate the choice that is correct and belongs in the blank. (**Note:** On the real GED® test, the choices will appear as a "drop-down" menu. When you click on a choice, it will appear in the blank.)*

    The U.S. Supreme Court has Select... ▼ justices, including the Chief Justice.

Select... ▼
five
seven
nine
eleven

54. *The following sentence contains blanks marked* Select... ▼. *Beneath each one is a set of choices. Indicate the choice that is correct and belongs in the blank. (**Note:** On the real GED® test, the choices will appear as a "drop-down" menu. When you click on a choice, it will appear in the blank.)*

In the event of the president's death or removal from office, the Select... ▼ becomes president. If that individual should

Select... ▼
vice president
Speaker of the House
Chief Justice of the Supreme Court

die in office, the next in line for the presidency is the Select... ▼

Select... ▼
vice president
Speaker of the House
Chief Justice of the Supreme Court

55. What is the purpose of a political party's national convention, held every four years?

A. to nominate candidates for president and vice president
B. to choose candidates for all the nation's governor seats
C. to determine the platform for the following year's election
D. to choose candidates for seats in the U.S. Congress

56. How many seats in the U.S. Senate are up for election every two years?

A. one-fifth
B. one-third
C. one-half
D. every seat

Questions 57–60 are based on the following maps, each of which lists the winner of the election on top in the lower right-hand corner:

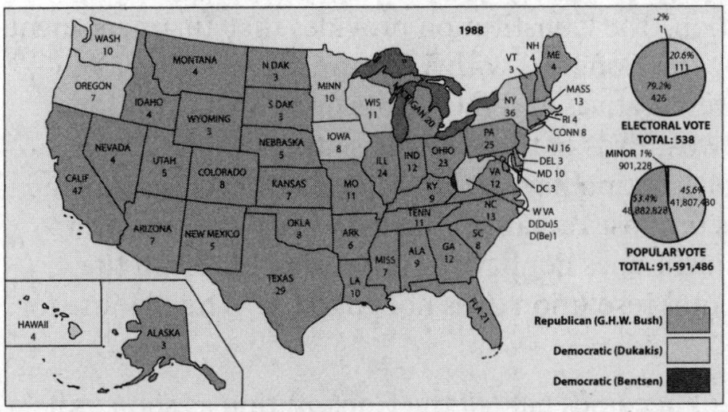

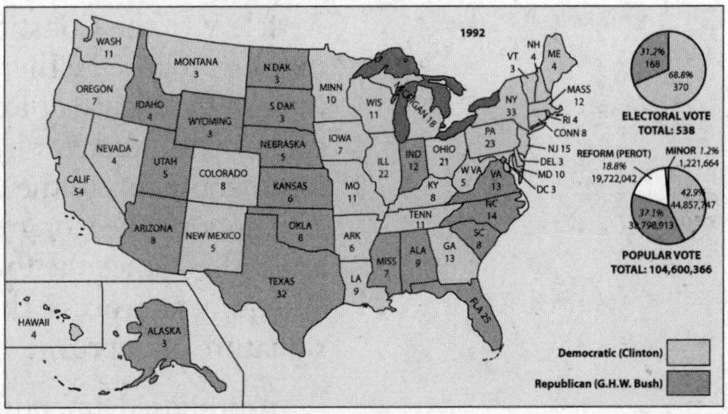

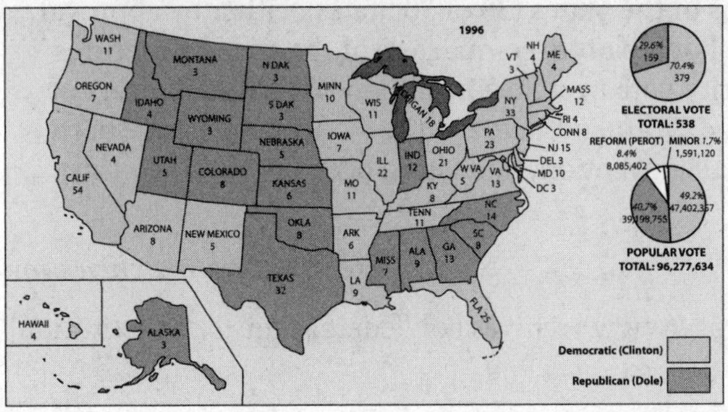

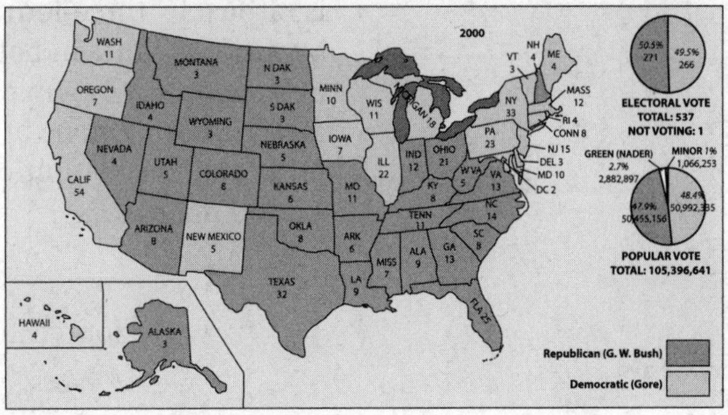

57. In which election did a third-party candidate have the most success?

    A. 1988
    B. 1992
    C. 1996
    D. 2000

58. In which election did the winner of the electoral vote not win a majority of the popular vote?

    A. 1988
    B. 1992
    C. 1996
    D. 2000

59. Which states were solidly Democratic in these four elections?

    A. California, Massachusetts, and Michigan
    B. Illinois, Iowa, and New York
    C. Minnesota, Nevada, and New Mexico
    D. Oregon, Washington, and Wisconsin

60. Which combination of states was solidly Republican in these four elections?

    A. Great Lakes states
    B. mid-Atlantic states
    C. New England states
    D. Texas and the Dakotas

Questions 61–62 are based on the following passage:

The authority to amend the Constitution of the United States is derived from Article V of the Constitution. The Constitution provides that an amendment may be proposed either by the Congress with a two-thirds majority vote in both the House of Representatives and the Senate or by a constitutional convention called for by two-thirds of the State legislatures. None of the 27 amendments to the Constitution have been proposed by constitutional convention. The Congress proposes an amendment in the form of a joint resolution. Since the President does not have a constitutional role in the amendment process, the joint resolution does not go to the White House for signature or approval.

A proposed amendment becomes part of the Constitution as soon as it is ratified by three-fourths of the States (38 of 50 States), either by approval by majority votes in both houses of three-quarters of the state legislatures or by approval by a majority vote in state conventions in three-quarters of all states. Since none of the 27 amendments to the Constitution have been proposed by constitutional convention, none have been approved by this second method.

Source: Excerpted from archives.gov

[Source: https://www.archives.gov/federal-register/constitution]

61. Which step has been followed in the case of every amendment that has been proposed for consideration to date?

    A. approval by special convention called by two-thirds of states
    B. approval by three-quarters of state legislatures
    C. approval by two-thirds majorities in both House and Senate
    D. approval by the president

62. Which statement is the *best* explanation of why the Founders who wrote the Constitution made the amendment process a two-step process and required supermajorities to approve each step?

    A. to make amending the Constitution difficult
    B. to make amending the Constitution impossible
    C. to keep the president from being involved in the process
    D. to ensure that citizens voted directly on all proposed amendments

Questions 63–65 are based on the following chart:

Country	Form of Government	Chief of State	Head of Government
Canada	federation; constitutional monarchy	British monarch	prime minister
China	communist state	president	premier
Germany	federal republic	president	chancellor
Iran	theocratic republic	supreme leader	president
Mexico	federal republic	president	president
Netherlands	constitutional monarchy	monarch	prime minister
Russia	federation	president	premier
Saudi Arabia	monarchy	king and prime minister	king and prime minister

Source: CIA World Factbook for each country.

63. Which country has a form of government most similar to that of the United States?

    A. Canada
    B. Germany
    C. Mexico
    D. Russia

64. Which country has the government in which one individual wields the most power?

    A. China
    B. Netherlands
    C. Russia
    D. Saudi Arabia

65. Which is the *best* explanation of what is meant by calling Iran a "theocratic state"?

    A. It is a dictatorship.
    B. Laws must conform to religious law.
    C. Laws must conform to constitutional theory.
    D. All officials must take an oath of office.

66. The census that is taken every ten years is used to determine what aspect of the federal government?

    A. the number of counties in each state
    B. the number of senators each state has
    C. the number of members each state has in the U.S. House
    D. the amount of federal revenue sharing each state receives

Questions 67–68 are based on the following passage from The Federalist Papers:

"The other point of difference is, the greater number of citizens and extent of territory which may be brought within the compass of republican than of democratic government; and it is this circumstance principally which renders factious combinations less to be dreaded in the former than in the latter. The smaller the society, the fewer probably will be the distinct parties and interests composing it; the fewer the distinct parties and interests, the more frequently will a majority be found of the same party; and the smaller the number of individuals composing a majority, and the smaller the compass within which they are placed, the more easily will they concert and execute their plans of oppression. Extend the sphere, and you take in a greater variety of parties and interests; you make it less probable that a majority of the whole will have a common motive to invade the rights of other citizens; or if such a common motive exists, it will be more difficult for all who feel it to discover their own strength, and to act in unison with each other."

—James Madison, *The Federalist,* No. 10

67. What does Madison say is the chief defense that a republican form of government provides against domination by a majority over the minority?

A. large size, which leads to the formation of many competing factions
B. greater likelihood of choosing wise and virtuous leaders
C. greater likelihood that citizens will agree on common goals
D. inability of factions or interest groups to form

68. Based on this passage, what does Madison mean by "factious combinations"?

A. small groups interested in destroying the state
B. political parties of any kind
C. groups of people with shared interests and goals
D. groups of representatives who work together

69. *The following sentence contains blanks marked* [*Select...* ▼]. *Beneath each one is a set of choices. Indicate the choice that is correct and belongs in the blank. (**Note:** On the real GED® test, the choices will appear as a "drop-down" menu. When you click on a choice, it will appear in the blank.)*

The U.S. House of Representatives has [Select... ▼] members, based on

Select... ▼
375
435
500

each state's population, and the U.S. Senate has [Select... ▼] members,

Select... ▼
50
100
150

with an equal number from each state.

Questions 70–72 are based on the following quotation, taken from a U.S. Supreme Court decision in the case United States v. Nixon, *in which President Richard Nixon claimed "executive privilege" should prevent him from turning over transcripts of conversations with aides, which had been requested in a criminal prosecution of one of his aides.*

"In this case, we must weigh the importance of the general privilege of confidentiality of Presidential communications in performance of the President's responsibilities against the inroads of such a privilege on the fair administration of criminal justice. The interest in preserving confidentiality is weighty indeed, and entitled to great respect. . . .

On the other hand, the allowance of the privilege to withhold evidence that is demonstrably relevant in a criminal trial would cut deeply into the guarantee of due process of law and gravely impair the basic function of the court. A President's acknowledged need for confidentiality in the communications of his office is general in nature, whereas the constitutional need for production of relevant evidence in a criminal proceeding is specific and central to the fair adjudication of a particular criminal case. . . .

We conclude that, when the ground for asserting privilege as to subpoenaed materials sought for use in a criminal trial is based only on the generalized interest in confidentiality, it cannot prevail over the fundamental demands of due process of law in the fair administration of criminal justice. The generalized assertion of privilege must yield to the demonstrated, specific need for evidence in a pending criminal trial."

—Chief Justice Warren Burger, *United States v. Nixon* (1974)

70. What position did the Court take regarding a president's right to claim "executive privilege" in general?

    A. There is no justification for the claim.
    B. The Constitution protects all executive conversations.
    C. The claim can be a valid one.
    D. Only top-secret conversations can be protected.

71. What constitutional issue did the Court's decision say conflicted with the claim of executive privilege?

    A. separation of powers
    B. due process
    C. free speech
    D. limited government

72. Based on the wording of this decision, what is reasonable to conclude that the Court ordered?

A. The president had to turn over the transcripts.
B. The president did not have to turn over the transcripts.
C. The Court had no jurisdiction in the case.
D. Further arguments were needed to decide the case.

Questions 73–75 are based on the following quotation from the Federal Bureau of Investigation website:

"The FBI focuses on threats that challenge the foundations of American society or involve dangers too large or complex for any local or state authority to handle alone. In executing the following priorities, the FBI—as both a national security and law enforcement organization—will produce and use intelligence to protect the nation from threats and to bring to justice those who violate the law.

1. Protect the United States from terrorist attack
2. Protect the United States against foreign intelligence operations and espionage
3. Protect the United States against cyber-based attacks and high-technology crimes
4. Combat public corruption at all levels
5. Protect civil rights
6. Combat transnational/national criminal organizations and enterprises
7. Combat major white-collar crime
8. Combat significant violent crime
9. Support federal, state, local and international partners
10. Upgrade technology to successfully perform the FBI's mission"

—Federal Bureau of Investigation, "Quick Facts"

73. What is the FBI's main mission?
    A. fighting local crime
    B. investigating government corruption
    C. ensuring civil rights are protected
    D. protecting the country and its people

74. Which mission would involve investigating a case of discrimination against members of a minority group?

    A. investigating white-collar crime
    B. combating violent crime
    C. protecting civil rights
    D. combating criminal organizations

75. Which mission would involve an investigation into a group of hackers breaking into a bank's computerized records?

    A. combating criminal organizations
    B. protecting against cyber-based attacks
    C. combating political corruption
    D. investigating white-collar crime

Questions 76–77 are based on the following diagram, which identifies the characteristics of a state, sometimes called a nation *or* country:

Four Characteristics of a National State

Population: people living in the state 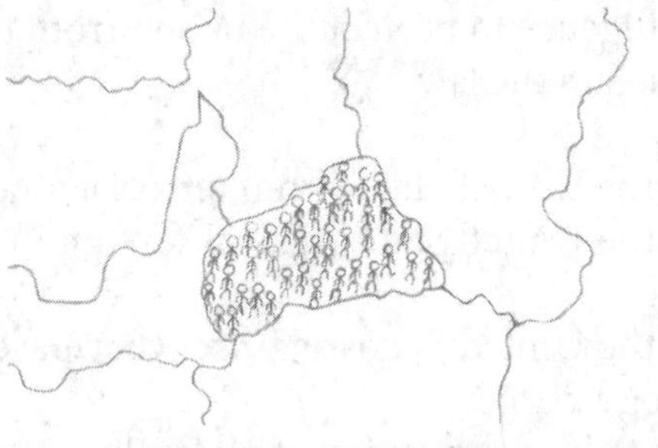	**Territory:** land that belongs to the state 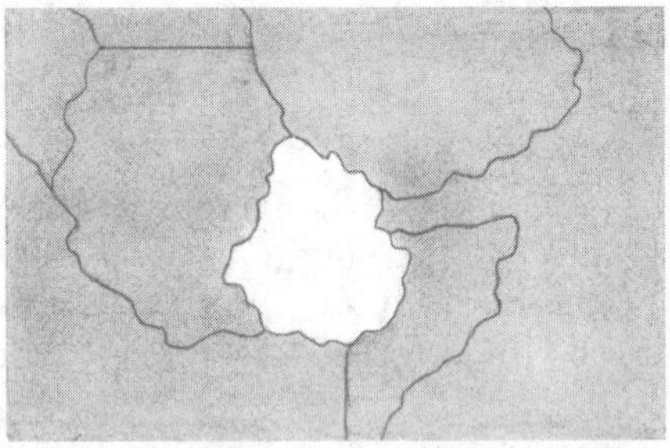
Sovereignty: the power to act independently within its own territory and in relations with other states 	**Government:** formal authority to make and carry out laws within the state 

76. Which characteristic of a national state does each of the fifty states within the United States lack?
    A. government
    B. population
    C. sovereignty
    D. territory

77. Aristotle, in his book *The Politics*, wrote that "the polity [or state] is a species of association" and that "if we go no further, its members must live in a common locality." To which of the characteristics of a state does this statement apply?
    A. government
    B. population
    C. sovereignty
    D. territory

78. *The following sentence contains a blank marked* Select... ▼. *Beneath it is a set of choices. Indicate the choice that is correct and belongs in the blank. (**Note:** On the real GED® test, the choices will appear as a "drop-down" menu. When you click on a choice, it will appear in the blank.)*

Before they can vote, people who are eligible to vote must Select... ▼

- register
- join a political party
- get a Social Security number

Questions 79–80 are based on the following quotation:

"It is emphatically the province and duty of the judicial department to say what the law is. Those who apply the rule to particular cases, must of necessity expound and interpret that rule. If two laws conflict with each other, the courts must decide on the operation of each. . . .

Thus, the particular phraseology of the constitution of the United States confirms and strengthens the principle, supposed to be essential to all written constitutions, that a law repugnant to the constitution is void; and that courts, as well as other departments, are bound by that instrument."

—Chief Justice John Marshall, *Marbury v. Madison* (1803)

79. What does Chief Justice Marshall mean in saying that "a law repugnant to the constitution is void"?

A. A federal law that contradicts state constitutions gives the federal government too much power.
B. A law that runs counter to the U.S. Constitution is not valid and need not be followed.
C. Citizens retain the right to break laws they consider invalid as a form of civil disobedience.
D. All laws have to be reviewed against the Constitution to determine if they reflect powers granted in that document.

80. The Supreme Court's decision in *Marbury v. Madison* established that the Supreme Court had the power to determine the constitutionality of acts of Congress. What is the term for that power?

A. judicial activism
B. judicial authority
C. judicial responsibility
D. judicial review

81. Which aspect of the U.S. Constitution contributes most to its being considered a living constitution?

A. the separation of powers
B. the federal system
C. the amendment process
D. the powers of the presidency

Questions 82–83 are based on the following passage:

There are four major types of Social Security benefits. The most common is retirement benefits, which are paid to retired workers who contributed to the Social Security system while they were working. To qualify for these benefits, workers must meet age eligibility requirements. Another type of Social Security benefit is disability, which is paid to workers who cannot work for at least 12 months because of illness or injury. These workers must meet eligibility requirements to qualify. Survivors' benefits are for widowed spouses, minor children, or dependent parents of individuals who were receiving retirement or disability benefits. They too must meet eligibility requirements. The final benefit type is called Supplemental Security Income, which is for disabled adults and children who have limited income. People must meet eligibility requirements to receive these benefits as well.

Source: Social Security Administration

82. Which type of benefit has age eligibility requirements?

    A. disability
    B. retirement
    C. Supplemental Security Income
    D. survivors

83. Which type of benefit would be received by the fully abled minor child of a deceased individual who had been retired?

    A. disability
    B. retirement
    C. Supplemental Security Income
    D. survivors

Questions 84–85 are based on the following diagram:

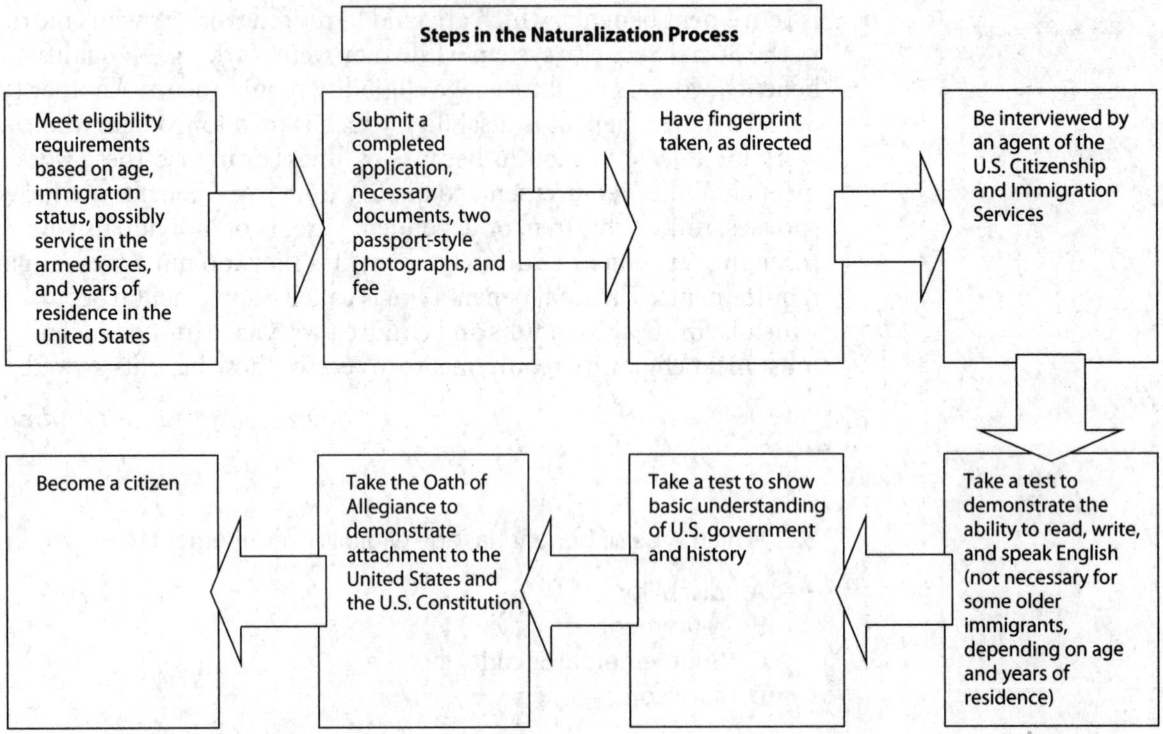

84. Which step in the naturalization process is optional for some individuals?

A. the interview
B. the application
C. taking the Oath of Allegiance
D. the English language test

85. Based on this diagram, for whom is the naturalization process intended?

A. undocumented immigrants
B. eligible immigrants who wish to become citizens
C. immigrants who join the armed forces
D. citizens who wish to register to vote

Questions 86–87 are based on the following diagram, which shows the structure of the executive branch of the federal government:

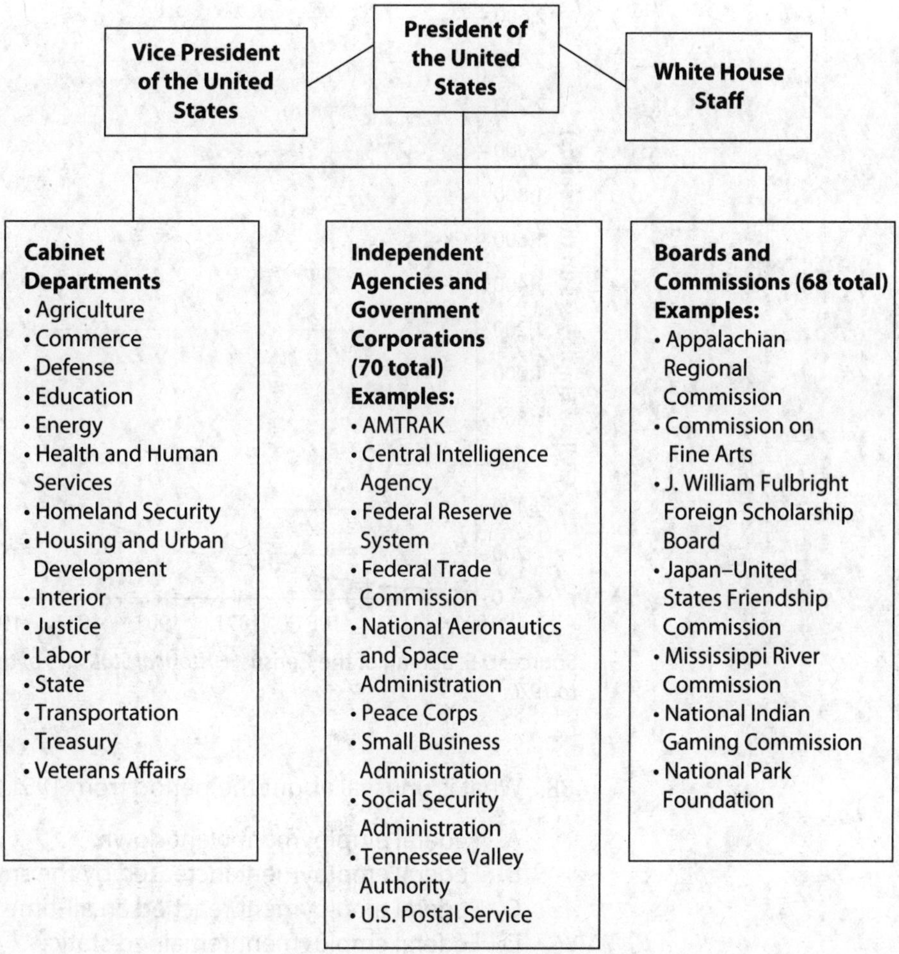

86. The president's chief of staff and press secretary are most likely found in which area of the organizational chart?

    A. boards and commissions
    B. cabinet departments
    C. independent agencies and government corporations
    D. White House staff

87. Which type of organization includes those with the greatest authority to act on their own?

    A. boards and commissions
    B. cabinet departments
    C. independent agencies and government corporations
    D. White House staff

Questions 88–89 are based on the following graph:

Source: U.S. Bureau of the Census, *Historical Statistics of the United States: Colonial Times to 1970.*

88. What is unusual about the period from 1951 to 1961?

    A. Federal employment went down.
    B. Federal employment increased by the smallest amount.
    C. Federal employment reached an all-time high.
    D. Federal employment remained static.

89. What inference can reasonably be made from the data in this graph?

    A. State and local governments were also increasing over this period.
    B. Growth of federal employment is due to growth in the armed forces.
    C. The federal government was providing more services over this period.
    D. Growth of the federal government after 1931 prompted the creation of the federal income tax.

Question 90 is based on the following excerpt from the Declaration of Independence.

"We hold these truths to be self-evident, that all men are created equal, that they are endowed by their Creator with certain unalienable Rights, that among these are life, liberty and the pursuit of happiness.—That to secure these rights, governments are instituted among men, deriving their just powers from the consent of the governed, —That whenever any form of government becomes destructive of these ends, it is the right of the people to alter or to abolish it, and to institute new government, laying its foundation on such principles and organizing its powers in such form, as to them shall seem most likely to effect their safety and happiness."

90. Which of the following ideas from the Magna Carta most likely influenced the ideas in this excerpt?

    A. the right to due process and trial by jury
    B. limitation on the taxation of citizens
    C. freedom of religion
    D. everyone being subject to the law

Question 91 is based on the following excerpt.

Excerpt from Jefferson's Draft for a Bill Establishing Religious Freedom (1777)

"We, the General Assembly of Virginia, do enact that no man shall be compelled to frequent or support any religious worship, place, or ministry whatsoever, nor shall be enforced, restrained, molested, or burdened in his body or goods, nor shall otherwise suffer, on account of his religious opinions or belief; but that all men shall be free to profess, and by argument to maintain, their opinions in matters of religion, and that the same shall in no wise diminish, enlarge, or affect their civil capacities."

The following sentence contains a blank marked [*Select...* ▼]. *Beneath the blank is a set of choices. Indicate the choice that is correct and belongs in the blank. (**Note:** On the real GED® test, the choices will appear as a "drop-down" menu. When you click on a choice, it will appear in the blank.)*

91. The [*Select...* ▼] amendment to the U.S. Constitution expresses these same ideas.

Select... ▼
First
Third
Fifth
Eighth

Question 92 is based on the following chart.

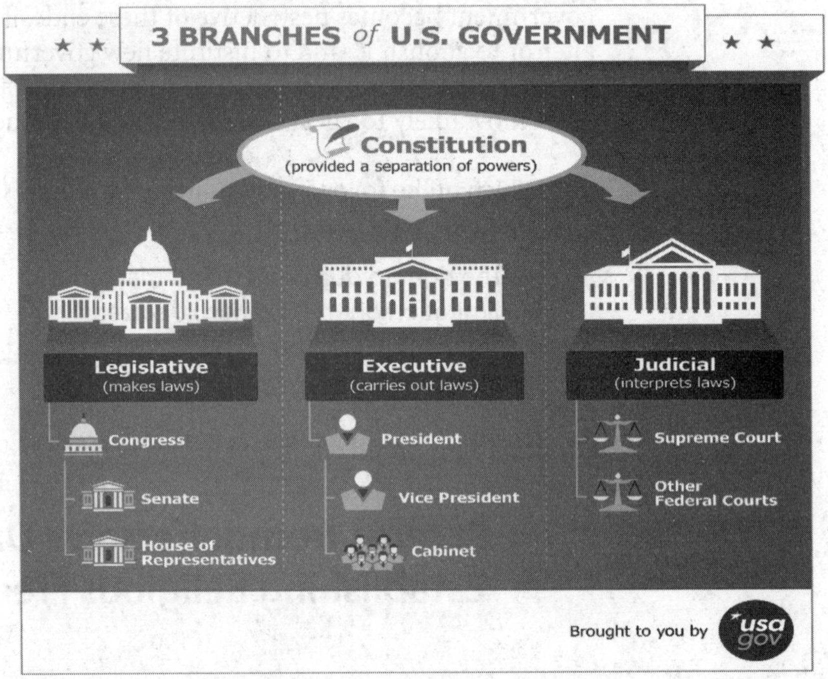

Source: https://www.usa.gov/branches-of-government.

92. Which of the following is a part of the executive branch?
   A. the Congressional Budget Office
   B. the U.S. Department of Energy
   C. the Court of Appeals for the Federal Circuit
   D. the House Office of Inspector General

Question 93 is based on the following two excerpts.

Excerpt from *Plessy v. Ferguson* (1896)

"The object of the [fourteenth] amendment was undoubtedly to enforce the absolute equality of the two races before the law, but, in the nature of things, it could not have been intended to abolish distinctions based upon color, or to enforce social, as distinguished from political, equality, or a commingling of the two races upon terms unsatisfactory to either. Laws permitting, and even requiring, their separation, in places where they are liable to be brought into contact, do not necessarily imply the inferiority of either race to the other, and have been generally, if not universally, recognized as within the competency of the state legislatures in the exercise of their police power."

Excerpt from *Brown v. Board of Education of Topeka* (1954)

"We come then to the question presented: does segregation of children in public schools solely on the basis of race, even though the physical facilities and other 'tangible' factors may be equal, deprive the children of the minority group of equal educational opportunities? We believe that it does . . . We conclude that, in the field of public education, the doctrine of 'separate but equal' has no place. Separate educational facilities are inherently unequal. Therefore, we hold that the plaintiffs and others similarly situated for whom the actions have been brought are, by reason of the segregation complained of, deprived of the equal protection of the laws guaranteed by the Fourteenth Amendment."

93. On which of the following matters did the two decisions differ?

    A. whether states have the right to make laws
    B. the definition of the word *equal*
    C. whether whites and blacks are inherently equal
    D. the validity of the Fourteenth Amendment

Question 94 is based on the following quote from the United States Oath of Allegiance.

"I hereby declare, on oath, that I absolutely and entirely renounce and abjure all allegiance and fidelity to any foreign prince, potentate, state, or sovereignty of whom or which I have heretofore been a subject or citizen; that I will support and defend the Constitution and laws of the United States of America against all enemies, foreign and domestic; that I will bear true faith and allegiance to the same; that I will bear arms on behalf of the United States when required by the law; that I will perform noncombatant service in the Armed Forces of the United States when required by the law; that I will perform work of national importance under civilian direction when required by the law; and that I take this obligation freely without any mental reservation or purpose of evasion; so help me God."

94. Which of the following promises does a person make when becoming a US citizen? Place an X on the blank next to each of your choices. (***Note:*** *On the real GED® test, you will click on the blank to put an X on it.*

    _______ to support the laws of the United States
    _______ to vote in presidential elections
    _______ to serve in the armed forces if called upon
    _______ to renounce allegiance to any foreign country

Question 95 is based on the following mission statement from the National Institutes of Health.

"NIH's mission is to seek fundamental knowledge about the nature and behavior of living systems and the application of that knowledge to enhance health, lengthen life, and reduce illness and disability."

95. Which of the following would be most consistent with the mission of the National Institutes of Health?

   A. researching the biological effects of environmental contaminants
   B. providing funding for research on capital punishment
   C. cleaning up contaminated land
   D. protecting and managing natural resources

Question 96 is based on the following information on how legislation is introduced.

"Beginning of a Bill: An idea for a bill may come from anybody, however only Members of Congress can introduce a bill in Congress. Bills can be introduced at any time the House is in session. There are four basic types of legislation: bills; joint resolutions; concurrent resolutions; and simple resolutions. A bill's type must be determined. A private bill affects a specific person or organization rather than the population at large. A public bill is one that affects the general public.

"Proposal of a Bill: After the idea for a bill is developed and the text of the bill is written, a Member of Congress must officially introduce the bill in Congress by becoming the bill's sponsor. Representatives usually sponsor bills that are important to them and their constituents. Representatives who sponsor bills will try to gain support for them, in hopes that they will become laws. Two or more sponsors for the same bill are called co-sponsors."

Source: https://lucas.house.gov/legislative-work/how-bill-becomes-law.

96. Place the following steps in the correct order. Indicate the box where each step belongs. (***Note:*** *On the real GED® test, you will click on each step and "drag" it into the correct box.)*

- a member of Congress sponsors the bill
- the text of the bill is written
- representatives work to gain support for the bill
- someone has an idea for a bill
- the bill's type is determined

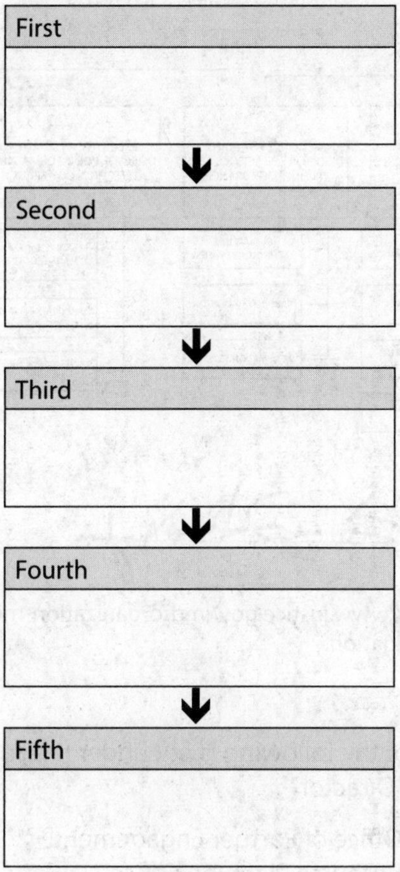

Question 97 is based on the following organizational chart from the Federal Bureau of Investigation.

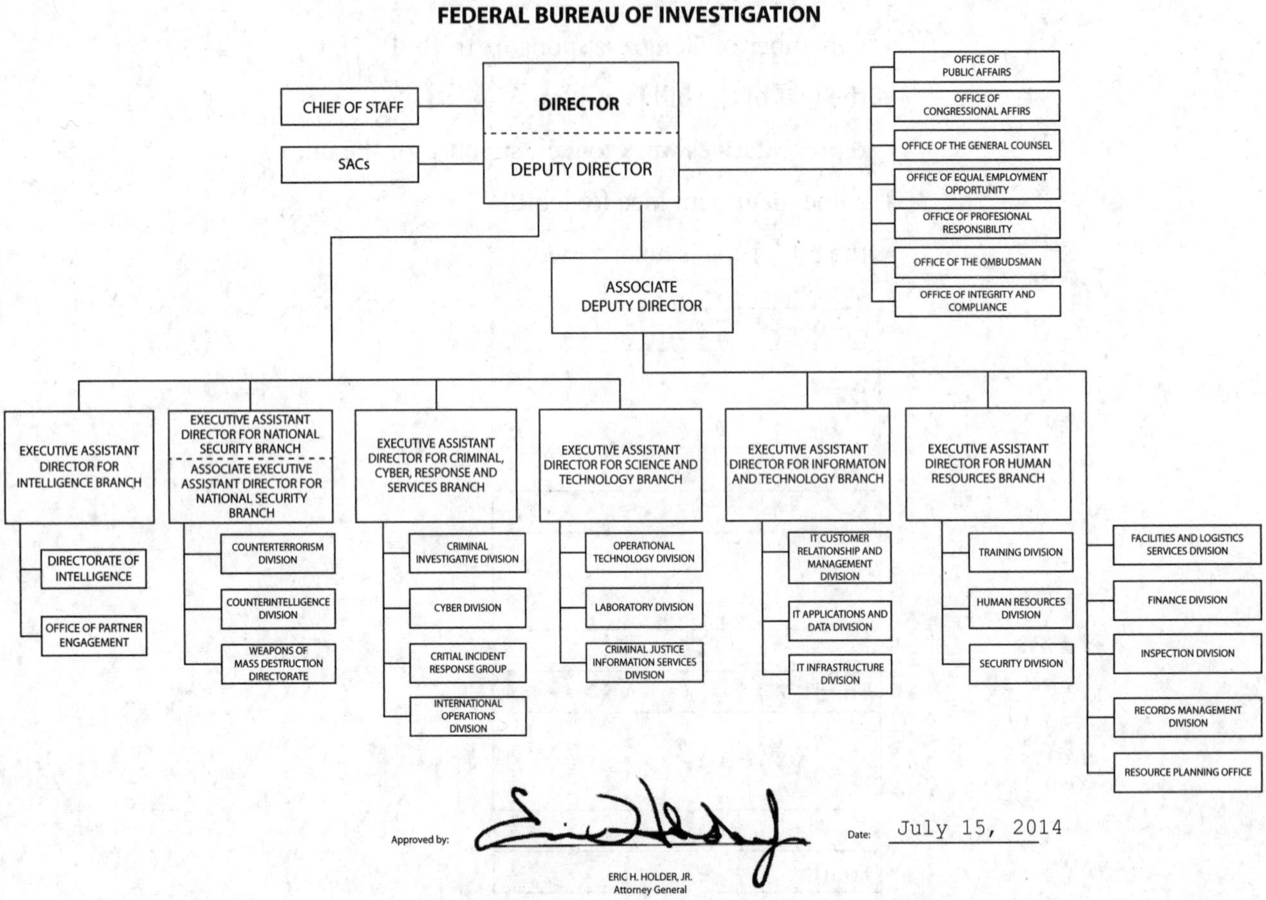

Source: https://www.justice.gov/jmd/organization-mission-and-functions-manual-federal-bureau-investigation.

97. Which of the following is *not* under the supervision of the Associate Deputy Director?

A. the Office of Partner Engagement
B. the Resource Planning Office
C. the Security Division
D. the Human Resources Division

Question 98 is based on the following New York voter registration card.

☐ Yes, I need an application for an Absentee ballot — **Please print or type in blue or black ink** — ☐ Yes, I would like to be an Election Day Worker

1	Are you a U.S. citizen? Yes ☐ No ☐ If you answered No, do not complete this form.	2	I will be 18 years old on or before election day: Yes ☐ No ☐ If you answered No, do not complete this form, unless you will be 18 by the end of the year.
3	Last Name / First Name / Middle Initial / Suffix		For Board use only!
4	Address Where You Live (do not give P.O. address) / Apt. No. / City/Town/Village / Zip Code / County		
5	Address Where You Get Your Mail (if different from above) / P.O. box, star rtc,. etc, / Post Office / Zip Code		
6	Date of Birth	7	Sex (circle) M F
8	Home Tel. Number (optional)	9	ID Number - Check the applicable box and provide your number ☐ New York Driver's License Number ☐ Last four digits of your Social Security number ➔ ☐ I do not have a New York Driver's License number of a Social Security number.
10	The last year you voted / Your Address was (give house number, street, and city) In county/state / Under the name (if different from your name now)		
11	**Choose a Party** — Check one box only ☐ REPUBLICAN PARTY ☐ DEMOCRATIC PARTY ☐ INDEPENDENCE PARTY ☐ CONSERVATIVE PARTY ☐ WORKING FAMILIES PARTY ☐ OTHER (writein) ____ ☐ I DO NOT WISH TO ENROLL IN A PARTY *Please note:* in order to vote in a **primary election,** you must be enrolled in one of these parties.	12	**AFFIDAVIT:** I swear or affirm that • I am a citizen of the United States. • I will have lived in the county, city, or village for at least 30 days before the election, • I meet all requirements to register to vote in New York State. • This is my signature or mark on the line below. • The above information is true. I understand that if it is not true I can be convicted and fined up to $5,000 and/or jailed for up to four years. ⬇ Signature or mark ⬇ X ____ Date

Please do not write in this space

Source: http://assembly.state.ny.us/comm/ELaw/20040210/form.html.

98. Which of the following people is not eligible to vote in New York?

A. a 19-year-old student
B. a person who is a naturalized U.S. citizen
C. a person who resides in New Jersey but works in New York
D. a person who holds public office in New York

Question 99 is based on the following information about jury eligibility.

To be legally qualified for jury service, an individual must:

- be a United States citizen;
- be at least 18 years of age;
- reside primarily in the judicial district for one year;
- be adequately proficient in English to satisfactorily complete the juror qualification form;
- have no disqualifying mental or physical condition;

- not currently be subject to felony charges punishable by imprisonment for more than one year; and
- never have been convicted of a felony (unless civil rights have been legally restored)

There are three groups that are exempt from federal jury service:

- members of the armed forces on active duty;
- members of professional fire and police departments; and
- "public officers" of federal, state, or local governments who are actively engaged full-time in the performance of public duties.

Persons employed on a full-time basis in any of these categories are barred from serving on federal juries, even if they desire to do so.

[Source: http://www.uscourts.gov/services-forms/jury-service/juror-qualifications.]

99. Which of the following people are not allowed to serve on a federal jury?

    A. a person who was previously convicted of a misdemeanor crime
    B. a person who works as a volunteer firefighter
    C. a retired U.S. Navy officer
    D. a person who works as a full-time police department dispatcher

100. Which of the following types of government would be most likely to hold a free and fair election to choose a leader?

    A. theocracy
    B. democracy
    C. monarchy
    D. oligarchy

THIS IS THE END OF CHAPTER 1: CIVICS AND GOVERNMENT.

CHAPTER 2

U.S. History

Directions: Answer the following questions. For multiple-choice questions, choose the best answer. For other questions, follow the directions preceding the question. Answers begin on page 174.

Questions 1–2 are based on the following quotation:

"We, whose names are underwritten, the Loyal Subjects of our dread sovereign lord King James, by the grace of God, of Great Britain, France, and Ireland, king, defender of the faith, [etcetera], having undertaken for the glory of God, and advancement of the Christian faith, and the honor of our king and country, a voyage to plant the first colony in the northern parts of Virginia; do. . . solemnly and mutually, in the presence of God and one another, covenant and combine ourselves together into a civil body politic, for our better ordering and preservation, and furtherance of the ends aforesaid: and by virtue hereof do enact, constitute, and frame, such just and equal laws, ordinances, acts, constitutions, and officers, from time to time, as shall be thought most meet and convenient for the general good of the colony; unto which we promise all due submission and obedience."

—from The Mayflower Compact (1620)

1. Which group of settlers wrote and signed this agreement in 1620?

   A. the English settlers of Jamestown, Virginia
   B. the Pilgrims who settled Plymouth, Massachusetts
   C. the Quakers who settled Pennsylvania
   D. the Catholics who settled Maryland

2. Why is this document considered a founding document in American self-government?

   A. The signers pledge to one another that they will form a civil government and obey its laws.
   B. The signers received the right to govern themselves by a charter granted by King James.
   C. It is the first formal constitution written in what became the United States.
   D. It is the first document establishing a government that was put to a popular vote.

3. The delegates at the Constitutional Convention agreed on three important compromises to resolve differences over the new government that they were creating under the Constitution. *Match each of the three compromises with the issue it resolved. Indicate the box where each compromise belongs. (**Note:** On the real GED® test, you will click on each compromise and "drag" it into the correct box.)*

Great Compromise	Three-Fifths Compromise	electoral college

Choosing the president	
Representation in Congress	
Counting enslaved people in population	

4. *Indicate the box where each characteristic of the Articles of Confederation belongs. (**Note:** On the real GED® test, you will click on each characteristic and "drag" it into the correct box.)*

taxation power	amending process
power to make treaties	court system
power to declare war	allowed formation of new states

Strength	
Weakness	

Questions 5–7 are based on the following map:

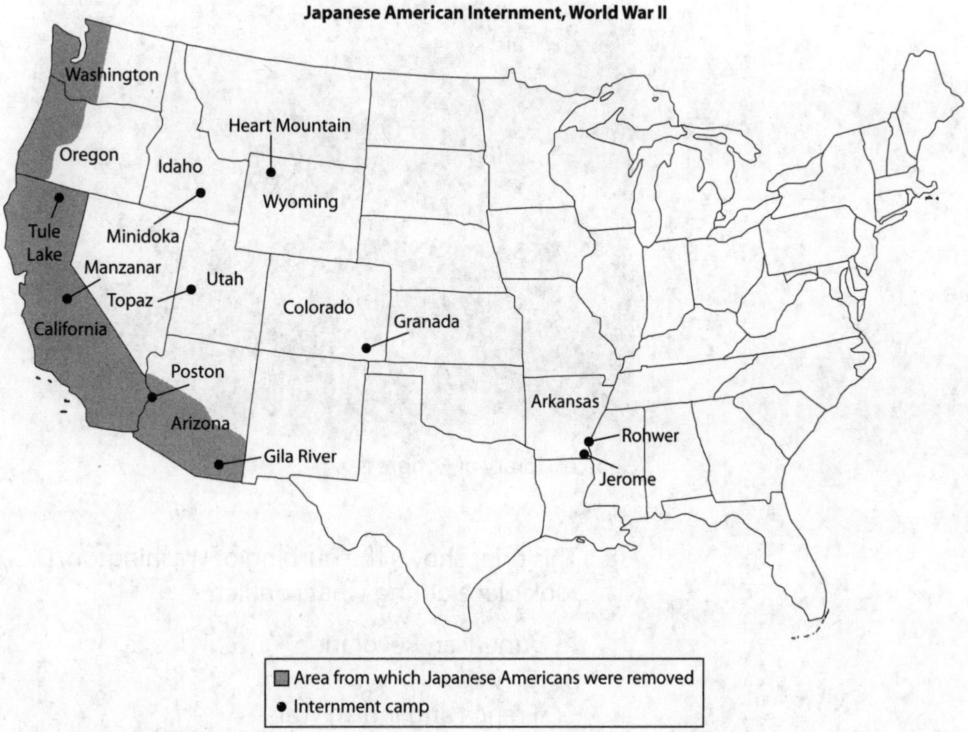

Source: National Park Service

5. Which of the following describes the internment of Japanese Americans during World War II?

   A. relocation from the coasts to the interior of the country
   B. relocation moved from the Mountain West to the West Coast
   C. relocation from the West Coast to the interior West and Southwest
   D. relocation from the East Coast to the West and West Coast

6. Which president issued Executive Order 9066, which led to the internment of Japanese Americans during World War II?

   A. Dwight D. Eisenhower
   B. Franklin D. Roosevelt
   C. Harry S Truman
   D. Woodrow Wilson

7. The placement of Japanese Americans in internment camps was most similar to what other action targeting a specific racial or ethnic group?

   A. segregation of African Americans
   B. reservation policy regarding Native Americans
   C. Bracero program for Mexican immigrants
   D. quota system for Eastern European immigrants

Question 8 is based on the following print:

Source: Library of Congress.

8. This print shows the burning of Washington, D.C., by British troops, which took place during what conflict?

   A. American Revolution
   B. Civil War
   C. French and Indian War
   D. War of 1812

Questions 9–10 are based on the following graph:

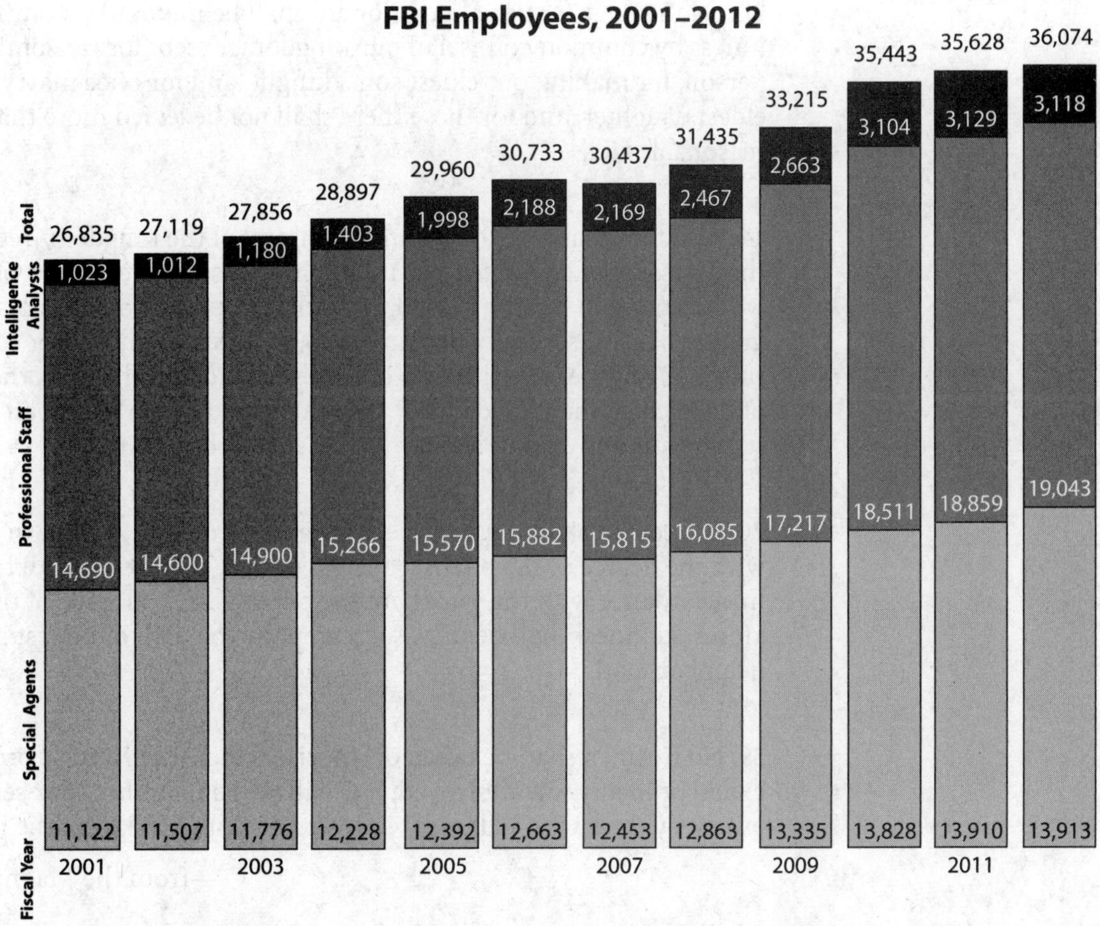

Source: U.S. Dept. of Justice.

9. In which fiscal year did the FBI most likely have funding cuts? *Write your answer in the blank.*

____

10. Which statement *best* explains the rise in employees dedicated to intelligence analysis in these years?

A. top priority given to investigating organized crime
B. sharp increase in illegal surveillance of Americans
C. growing emphasis on fighting terrorism
D. shift from field agents to analysts

Questions 11–13 are based on the following quotation:

"12. No scutage [a special tax] nor aid shall be imposed on our kingdom, unless by common counsel of our kingdom, except for ransoming our person, for making our eldest son a knight, and for once marrying our eldest daughter; and for these there shall not be levied more than a reasonable aid. . . .

14. And for obtaining the common counsel of the kingdom [regarding] the assessing of an aid (except in the three cases aforesaid) or of a scutage, we will cause to be summoned the archbishops, bishops, abbots, earls, and greater barons, severally by our letters; and we will moreover cause to be summoned generally, through our sheriffs and bailiffs, and others who hold of us in chief, for a fixed date . . . and at a fixed place; and in all letters of such summons we will specify the reason of the summons. . . .

20. A freeman shall not be [fined] for a slight offense, except in accordance with the degree of the offense; and for a grave offense he shall be [fined] in accordance with the gravity of the offense, . . . and none of the aforesaid [fines] shall be imposed except by the oath of honest men of the neighborhood.

39. No freemen shall be taken or imprisoned or [deprived of property] or exiled or in any way destroyed, nor will we go upon him nor send upon him, except by the lawful judgment of his peers or by the law of the land."

—from the Magna Carta (1215)

11. *The following sentence contains blanks marked* Select... ▼. *Beneath each one is a set of choices. Indicate the choice that is correct and belongs in the blank. (**Note:** On the real GED® test, the choices will appear as a "drop-down" menu. When you click on a choice, it will appear in the blank.)*

The first two clauses quoted in this excerpt address issues of Select... ▼.

Select... ▼
popular votes
taxation
property rights

The second two clauses address the issues of Select... ▼

Select... ▼
crime and punishment
personal rights
property rights

12. What principle underlying American democracy does the Magna Carta represent, as shown in these passages?
    A. federalism
    B. minority rights
    C. representative government
    D. rule of law

13. Which statement is an appropriate paraphrase for the text of clause 20?
    A. There shall be no taxation without representation.
    B. All men are created equal.
    C. The punishment should fit the crime.
    D. All accused must be tried by a jury of their peers.

14. *Place the documents in the correct order, from oldest to most recent. Indicate the box where each document belongs. (**Note:** On the real GED® test, you will click on each document name and "drag" it into the correct box.)*

U.S. Constitution	English Bill of Rights	Mayflower Compact
Magna Carta	Declaration of Independence	

First

↓

Second

↓

Third

↓

Fourth

↓

Fifth

Questions 15–18 are based on the following chart:

Legal Immigrants Entering the United States, by Region, 1830–2009

	1830 to 1839	1840 to 1849	1850 to 1859	1860 to 1869	1870 to 1879	1880 to 1889	1890 to 1899	1900 to 1909	1910 to 1919	1920 to 1929
Europe	422,853	1,369,423	2,622,617	1,880,389	2,252,050	4,638,684	3,576,411	7,572,569	4,985,411	2,560,340
Asia	55	121	36,080	54,408	134,071	71,152	61,304	300,441	269,736	126,740
Americas	31,911	50,527	84,201	130,427	345,889	529,845	38,756	277,882	1,070,539	1,591,278
Africa	66	67	104	458	441	768	432	6,326	8,867	6,362
Oceania	54	61	92	328	297	567	354	11,677	12,339	5,299

Source: U.S. Dept. of Homeland Security.

15. Which region provided the greatest share of immigrants who were legal residents in the decades shown on this chart?

A. Africa
B. Americas
C. Asia
D. Europe

16. About how many immigrants came as legal residents from Europe in the decades from 1880 to 1919?

A. about 10 million
B. about 15 million
C. about 20 million
D. about 30 million

17. Immigration from China was growing in the 1800s until the passage of the Chinese Exclusion Act, which barred most Chinese from coming to the United States. Based on the chart, in which decade was that law likely passed?

A. 1860–1869
B. 1870–1879
C. 1880–1889
D. 1900–1909

18. In which decade can you reasonably infer that new immigration laws were passed as a reaction to several decades of high immigration from Eastern and Southern Europe?

A. 1860–1869
B. 1890–1899
C. 1900–1909
D. 1920–1929

19. *Match the name of each major American war with its time span and the names of the opposing sides. Indicate the box where each item belongs. (**Note:** On the real GED® test, you will click on each item and "drag" it into the correct box.)*

Britain and United States	1914–1918	United Nations and Axis
1812–1815	North and South	Allied and Central Powers
1939–1945	1861–1865	

War of 1812	Civil War

World War I	World War II

20. The Great Compromise, reached during the Constitutional Convention, resolved a sharp disagreement about representation in Congress between what two groups?

    A. large states and small states
    B. slave states and free states
    C. new states and original states
    D. federalist and anti-federalist states

Questions 21–23 are based on the following map:

Europe in the Cold War

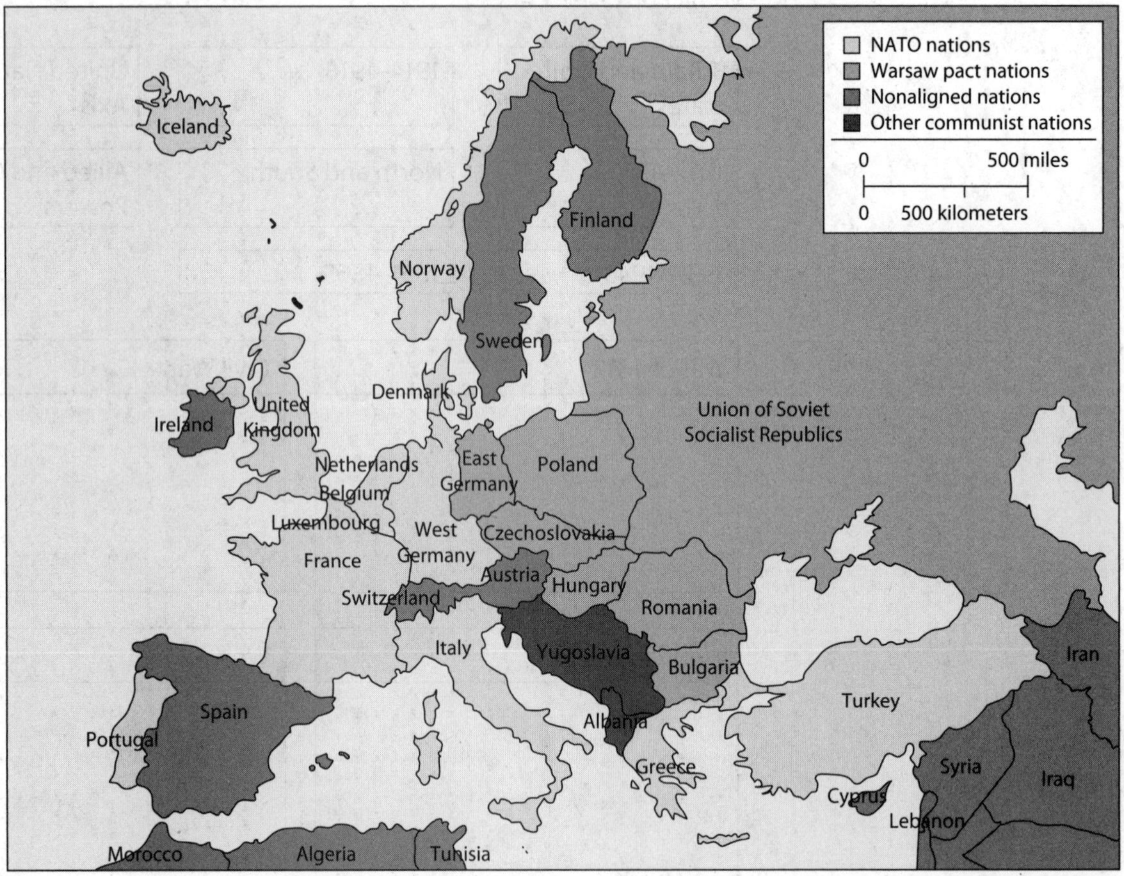

21. Which communist state was not part of the Warsaw Pact?
    A. Czechoslovakia
    B. East Germany
    C. Romania
    D. Yugoslavia

22. What member of NATO does not appear on the map because it is not located in Europe?
    A. Australia
    B. Mexico
    C. New Zealand
    D. United States

23. What can you infer about the governments of the "nonaligned nations" such as Finland and Sweden?
    A. They were led by socialist parties.
    B. They did not have communist governments.
    C. They were constitutional monarchies.
    D. They had no standing armies.

Questions 24–25 are based on the following quotation:

"When in the course of human events, it becomes necessary for one people to dissolve the political bands which have connected them with another, and to assume among the powers of the earth, the separate and equal station to which the laws of nature and of nature's God entitle them, a decent respect to the opinions of mankind requires that they should declare the causes which impel them to the separation.

We hold these truths to be self-evident, that all men are created equal, that they are endowed by their Creator with certain unalienable Rights, that among these are life, liberty and the pursuit of happiness. —That to secure these rights, governments are instituted among men, deriving their just powers from the consent of the governed, —That whenever any form of government becomes destructive of these ends, it is the right of the people to alter or to abolish it, and to institute new government, laying its foundation on such principles and organizing its powers in such form, as to them shall seem most likely to effect their safety and happiness."

—Declaration of Independence (1776)

24. Which principle established by Enlightenment political thinkers does the Declaration of Independence use in this passage to justify rebellion against Great Britain?

    A. sovereignty of the people; natural rights
    B. equality of all people; religious toleration
    C. no taxation without representation; abolition of slavery
    D. republican government; equal justice

25. What is the purpose of the Declaration of Independence, according to the first paragraph in this excerpt?

    A. to complain about the king's tyranny
    B. to demand representation in Parliament
    C. to justify the rebellion
    D. to demand an end to unfair taxation

Questions 26–28 are based on the following chart:

Alliance System Before World War I

Country	Alliance	Other Notes
Austria-Hungary	Triple Alliance	Faced nationalist unrest in the Balkans; feared growth of Serbia
Belgium	none (neutral)	Britain and France promised to defend it if invaded
France	Triple Entente	Resented defeat by Germany in Franco-Prussian War of 1870
Germany	Triple Alliance	Faced possibility of war on west and east
Great Britain	Triple Entente	Engaged in naval arms race with Germany
Italy	Triple Alliance	Had secret treaty with France requiring it to not fight if Germany attacked France; joined Allies in 1915
Ottoman Empire	none	Rival with Russia in Balkans, Black Sea; joined Central Powers after war broke out
Russia	Triple Entente	Wanted more influence in Balkans
Serbia	with Russia	Was growing in early 1910s, threatening Austria-Hungary's hold on the Balkans

26. Which member of the Triple Alliance could not be entirely counted on if war broke out?

    A. Austria-Hungary
    B. Germany
    C. Italy
    D. Russia

27. What two countries were most likely to be embroiled in war first if conflict broke out in Serbia?

    A. Austria-Hungary and Russia
    B. France and Germany
    C. Italy and Germany
    D. the Ottoman Empire and Great Britain

28. What danger was posed to peace in Europe by the alliance system that existed before World War I?

    A. France was geographically isolated and without strong allies.
    B. Germans were angry over the punishing peace from the previous war.
    C. A local war could quickly become a war involving the whole continent.
    D. Austria-Hungary was threatened by nationalist unrest.

29. Which of the following actions was a decisive factor in the American Revolution?

A. the departure of tens of thousands of Loyalists
B. the betrayal of Benedict Arnold
C. the British capture of Philadelphia
D. France's agreement to ally with the Patriots

30. *Match each of the Civil War Constitutional amendments with one of the results in the list. Indicate the box where each result belongs. (**Note:** On the real GED® test, you will click on each result and "drag" it into the correct box.)*

abolition of slavery	citizenship for African Americans
suffrage for African American males	

Thirteenth Amendment	Fourteenth Amendment

Fifteenth Amendment

Questions 31–32 are based on the following quotation:

"It is now time for the opposition to the annexation of Texas to cease, all further agitation of the waters of bitterness and strife, at least in connection with this question,—even though it may perhaps be required of us as a necessary condition of the freedom of our institutions, that we must live on forever in a state of unpausing struggle and excitement upon some subject of party division or other. But, in regard to Texas, enough has now been given to party. It is time for the common duty of patriotism to the country to succeed;—or if this claim will not be recognized, it is at least time for common sense to acquiesce with decent grace in the inevitable and the irrevocable. . . .

Why, were other reasoning wanting, in favor of now elevating this question of the reception of Texas into the Union, out of the lower region of our past party dissensions, up to its proper level of a high and broad nationality, it surely is to be found, found abundantly, in the manner in which other nations have undertaken to intrude themselves into it, . . . in a spirit of hostile interference against us, for the avowed object of thwarting our policy and hampering our power, limiting our greatness and checking the fulfillment of our manifest destiny to overspread the continent allotted by Providence for the free development of our yearly multiplying millions."

—John L. O'Sullivan, "Annexation," *The United States Magazine and Democratic Review* (1845)

31. What can be inferred about the question of the annexation of Texas from this passage?

    A. The issue had split the country on partisan grounds.
    B. The issue had split the country on class grounds.
    C. The American people were almost unanimously in favor of annexation.
    D. Fear that annexation would result in a civil war was widespread.

32. What did O'Sullivan mean when he wrote of the "manifest destiny" of the United States?

    A. the inevitability that slavery would plunge North and South into a civil war
    B. the idea that the United States was uniquely destined to lead the world
    C. the certain victory of the United States over the Soviet Union in the Cold War
    D. the right of the United States to expand across the continent of North America

33. Which president resigned under threat of impeachment for his actions in the Watergate scandal?

A. Bill Clinton
B. Ulysses Grant
C. Andrew Johnson
D. Richard Nixon

34. *Match each of the achievements in the list with one of the two early leaders of the United States. Indicate the box where each achievement belongs. (**Note:** On the real GED® test, you will click on each achievement and "drag" it into the correct box.)*

served as first president	wrote Declaration of Independence
made Louisiana Purchase	commander of Continental Army
president of Constitutional Convention	

George Washington	Thomas Jefferson

Questions 35–36 are based on the following passage:

"In every stage of these oppressions we have petitioned for redress in the most humble terms: Our repeated petitions have been answered only by repeated injury. A prince whose character is thus marked by every act which may define a tyrant, is unfit to be the ruler of a free people.

Nor have we been wanting in attentions to our British brethren. We have warned them from time to time of attempts by their legislature to extend an unwarrantable jurisdiction over us. We have reminded them of the circumstances of our emigration and settlement here. We have appealed to their native justice and magnanimity, and we have conjured them by the ties of our common kindred to disavow these usurpations, which, would inevitably interrupt our connections and correspondence. They too have been deaf to the voice of justice and of consanguinity. We must, therefore, acquiesce in the necessity, which denounces our separation, and hold them, as we hold the rest of mankind, enemies in war, in peace friends."

—Declaration of Independence (1776)

35. Which of the following is a paraphrase of these two paragraphs from the Declaration of Independence, which follow the list of grievances against the king and Parliament?

    A. As humans possessing basic natural rights, we have the right to form our own government.
    B. That government is best which governs least, so we want limited government.
    C. We tried to resolve our grievances peacefully, but received only harsh treatment in response.
    D. We will never be reconciled with the British people after their unjust treatment of us.

36. Which phrase is used to justify the Americans' characterization of the king's and Parliament's actions as "usurpations"?

    A. "petitioned for redress"
    B. "appealed to their native justice and magnanimity"
    C. "deaf to the voice of justice and consanguinity"
    D. "extend an unwarrantable jurisdiction"

37. The president at the time of the Watergate scandal lost political support because of his involvement in what activity?

    A. abuse of power and obstruction of justice after a burglary
    B. accepting money in exchange for the appointment of new ambassadors
    C. conflict over the policy to follow in Reconstruction
    D. obstruction of justice after a sex scandal

38. Why did Congress enact a law in 1867 ordering the military occupation of the South?

    A. to combat the formation of the Confederate States of America
    B. to enforce the Fourteenth and Fifteenth Amendments
    C. in response to the passage of "black codes" that limited the rights of former enslaved persons
    D. in response to widespread, ongoing raids by Native Americans on southern cities

39. The following is a list of characteristics of the North and South regions of the United States before the Civil War. *Indicate the box where each characteristic belongs. (**Note:** On the real GED® test, you will click on each characteristic and "drag" it into the correct box.)*

slave labor	growing industry	immigration
plantation economy	high tariffs	free labor
growth of Republican Party	low tariffs	opposition to abolition
states' rights	permanency of the Union	

North	South

Questions 40–42 are based on the following passage:

"At the present moment in world history nearly every nation must choose between alternative ways of life. The choice is too often not a free one.

One way of life is based upon the will of the majority, and is distinguished by free institutions, representative government, free elections, guarantees of individual liberty, freedom of speech and religion, and freedom from political oppression.

The second way of life is based upon the will of a minority forcibly imposed upon the majority. It relies upon terror and oppression, a controlled press and radio; fixed elections, and the suppression of personal freedoms.

I believe that it must be the policy of the United States to support free peoples who are resisting attempted subjugation by armed minorities or by outside pressures.

I believe that we must assist free peoples to work out their own destinies in their own way.

I believe that our help should be primarily through economic and financial aid which is essential to economic stability and orderly political processes."

—Harry S Truman, address to Congress (1947)

40. In this speech, which introduced the Truman Doctrine, President Harry Truman outlined the fundamental differences that divided which two sides?

    A. Allies and fascist powers
    B. the United States and Soviet Union
    C. North and South
    D. free democracies and terrorist organizations

41. Truman's speech led to his adoption of what Cold War policy, which was followed by subsequent presidents?

    A. containment, or attempts to prevent communist expansion
    B. détente, or cooperation with the Soviet Union
    C. intervention, or American involvement in the Vietnam War
    D. anticolonialism, or U.S. support for the independence of European-held colonies

42. Which action was adopted soon after Truman's speech in part to implement his new policy?

    A. the space race
    B. escalation in Vietnam
    C. the Marshall Plan
    D. expansion of NATO

Questions 43–45 are based on the following quotation:

"When one surveys the world about him after the great storm, noting the marks of destruction and yet rejoicing in the ruggedness of the things which withstood it, if he is an American he breathes the clarified atmosphere with a strange mingling of regret and new hope. We have seen a world passion spend its fury, but we contemplate our Republic unshaken, and hold our civilization secure. . . .

The recorded progress of our Republic, materially and spiritually, in itself proves the wisdom of the inherited policy of noninvolvement in Old World affairs. Confident of our ability to work out our own destiny, and jealously guarding our right to do so, we seek no part in directing the destinies of the Old World. We do not mean to be entangled. We will accept no responsibility except as our own conscience and judgment, in each instance, may determine.

Our eyes never will be blind to a developing menace, our ears never deaf to the call of civilization. We recognize the new order in the world, with the closer contacts which progress has wrought. We sense the call of the human heart for fellowship, fraternity, and cooperation. We crave friendship and harbor no hate. But America, our America, the America builded on the foundation laid by the inspired fathers, can be a party to no permanent military alliance. It can enter into no political commitments, nor assume any economic obligations which will subject our decisions to any other than our own authority."

—Warren G. Harding, Inaugural Address (1921)

43. What foreign policy position is represented by Harding's stated aim of avoiding any military alliances or political "entanglements" with other nations?

    A. American exceptionalism
    B. containment
    C. interventionism
    D. isolationism

44. Harding's position is in part a reaction to the recent termination of what event, which he called "the great storm" and said was marked by "destruction" and a "world passion spend[ing] its fury"?

    A. the French Revolution
    B. World War I
    C. World War II
    D. the Cold War

45. Harding states that the United States should "enter into no political commitments, nor assume any economic obligations which will subject our decisions to any other than our own authority." This position is similar to what modern foreign policy debate?

    A. the war on terrorism
    B. immigration control
    C. influence of the United Nations
    D. free trade agreements

Questions 46–48 are based on the following timeline:

1955	**1955–1956**	African Americans stage Montgomery bus boycott, win end to segregation in public transportation; Martin Luther King Jr. emerges as leader
	1957	Martin Luther King Jr. and other clergy found Southern Christian Leadership Conference to promote nonviolent protest
1960	**1960**	Activists, including SNCC members, stage sit-ins that result in retailers ending segregation in restaurants
	1961	CORE and SNCC stage Freedom Rides to push government to enforce Court decision ending segregation in interstate travel
	1963	Martin Luther King Jr. argues in "Letter from a Birmingham Jail" that African Americans have a right to push for equality now; hundreds of thousands march on Washington, D.C., to push for civil rights
	1964	Congress passes Civil Rights Act banning discrimination in many public settings; SNCC stages "Freedom Summer" in Mississippi to register African American voters
1965	**1965**	Police beat demonstrators at march in Selma, Alabama; Congress passes Voting Rights Act to enforce voting rights for African Americans

46. Which of these would be the *most* appropriate title for this timeline?

   A. The Turbulent 1950s and 1960s
   B. Milestones of the Civil Rights Movement
   C. The Triumph of Segregation
   D. Martin Luther King's Legacy

47. What event most likely prompted Martin Luther King Jr. to write his "Letter from a Birmingham Jail"?

   A. Congress's ongoing debate over the Voting Rights Act
   B. success of the Montgomery bus boycott
   C. criticism of the urgency of the demands from civil rights activists
   D. founding of the Southern Christian Leadership Conference

48. Which event most likely pushed Congress to pass the Voting Rights Act of 1965?

   A. Freedom Summer
   B. Freedom Rides
   C. Montgomery bus boycott
   D. sit-ins

Question 49 is based on the following photograph taken during the Berlin Airlift:

Source: Library of Congress.

49. What was the purpose of this airlift?

    A. to provide arms to German resistance fighters during World War II
    B. to bring supplies to blockaded West Berlin during the Cold War
    C. to strengthen advocates of peace in the last months of World War I
    D. to deliver food and clothing to survivors of the Holocaust

Questions 50–51 are based on the following passage.

During World War II, the Nazi government of Germany committed a horrific act: the murder by quasi-industrial processes of some 6 million European Jews who were deemed inferior. The Jews were stripped of their property, forced into ghettos, and eventually transported to camps, mainly in the occupied countries to the east of Germany, where they were systematically put to death. Huge numbers of other groups, such as prisoners of war and people with mental illnesses, were also murdered, but the murder of the Jews was different in that it was an attempt to exterminate an entire population.

50. What name is used to describe the murder of 6 million European Jews by the Nazi government of Germany during World War II?

    A. anti-Semitism
    B. the Crusades
    C. the Holocaust
    D. the Resistance

51. What development of the postwar world is in major part a result of the Nazis' action?

    A. the founding of the state of Israel
    B. the Cold War
    C. the founding of the United Nations
    D. decolonization

52. The items in the following list refer either to segregation or desegregation in the American South. *Indicate the box where each item belongs. (**Note:** On the real GED® test, you will click on each item and "drag" it into the correct box.)*

Jim Crow laws	*Brown v. Board of Education*
Civil Rights Act of 1964	*Plessy v. Ferguson*
NAACP	Ku Klux Klan

Segregation	Desegregation

Questions 53–54 are based on the following map:

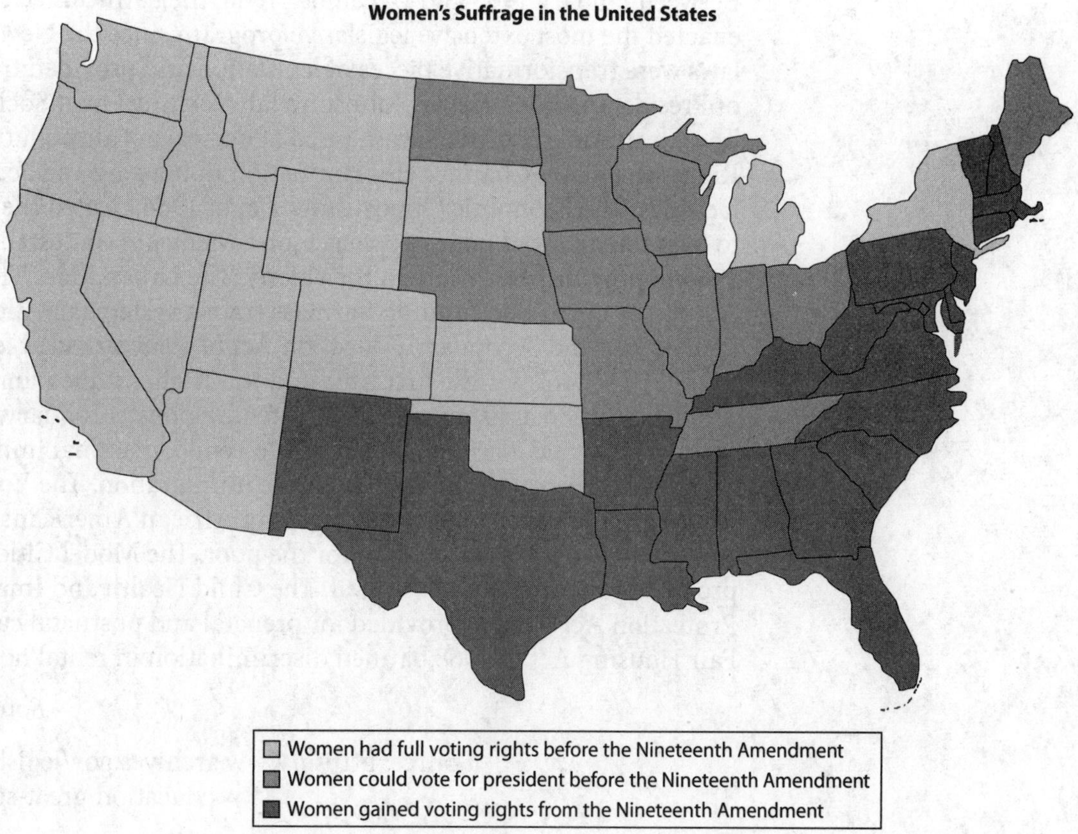

53. In which state could a woman vote in a presidential election but not in state or local elections before ratification of the Nineteenth Amendment? *Write your answer in the blank.*

____

54. Which generalization can be made about women's voting rights based on this map?

   A. Women had full or partial voting rights in nearly two-thirds of the states before the Nineteenth Amendment.
   B. Ratification of the Nineteenth Amendment gave voting rights for the first time to American women.
   C. The older states of the east and south were most resistant to granting women's suffrage.
   D. The granting of women's suffrage was a gradual process that took many decades.

Questions 55–56 are based on the following passage:

Between January 1965 and December 1966, the 89th United States Congress enacted the most extensive legislative program since the New Deal. These laws were transformative pieces of legislation and provided the cornerstone of President Lyndon Baines Johnson's far-reaching Great Society agenda. The Clean Air Act of 1963 was aimed at decreasing air pollution. The Civil Rights Act of 1964 banned discrimination in housing and access to public facilities. The Economic Opportunity Act of 1964 created the Job Corps to help unemployed poor people get jobs. Medicare was established in 1964 to provide health care to the elderly. The Urban Mass Transportation Act of 1964 provided funding for mass transit systems in cities. The Elementary and Secondary Education Act of 1965 provided federal funding for public schools for the first time and the Higher Education Act of 1965 provided tuition assistance to those attending postsecondary schools. The Immigration and Nationality Act of 1965 ended national immigration quotas and opened the country to more immigration. The Voting Rights Act of 1965 protected the voting rights of African Americans. The Medicaid Act of 1966 ensured health care for the poor. The Model Cities Act of 1966 provided funds for urban renewal. The Child Health and Improvement and Protection Act of 1968 provided for prenatal and postnatal care. Finally, the Fair Housing Act of 1968 banned discrimination in rental housing.

—*Source: archives.gov*

[Source: https://www.archives.gov/legislative/resources/education/great-society-congress]

55. Based on this list of legislation, what can you conclude was the overall goal of Lyndon Johnson's Great Society program?

    A. to improve society by helping the poor, children, and the elderly
    B. to rescue the economy from collapse
    C. to win a propaganda victory in the Cold War
    D. to unleash market forces by lessening government involvement in the economy

56. What was a likely result of this legislation?

    A. an end to poverty
    B. an end to racial discrimination
    C. increased social unrest
    D. increased size of the federal government

Questions 57–59 are based on the following diagram, which details three of the factors that helped contribute to the outbreak of World War I:

Causes of World War I

Imperialism	Nationalism	Militarism
• Scramble for colonies in Africa and Asia • Competition for raw materials and new markets	• Exaltation of the ethnic-based nation-state • Sense of grievances (French desire to punish Germany for French defeat in Franco-Prussian War) • Desire for autonomy among ethnic groups in multiethnic empires • Used by conservative governments to reduce class resentments	• Arms race among great powers • Culture that glorified military • Absence of major war since early 1800s

57. Unrest in the Balkans against Austria-Hungary is an example of which of these causative factors?
    A. arms race among great powers
    B. desire for autonomous ethnic states within multiethnic empires
    C. scramble for colonies in Africa
    D. competition for raw materials and new markets

58. The competition between Britain and Germany to have the larger fleet and the most battleships was an example of which of these causative factors?
    A. arms race among great powers
    B. competition for raw materials and new markets
    C. sense of grievances
    D. scramble for colonies in Africa and Asia

59. How were imperialism and nationalism connected?
    A. Imperialism reduced the effectiveness of efforts to reduce class conflict.
    B. Imperialism fed the glorification of military virtues.
    C. Addition of new colonies fed national pride.
    D. Obtaining new markets enhanced the success of nationalized industries.

Questions 60–61 are based on the following timeline:

1988
- **July**: Mass protests in Baltic states (Lithuania, Latvia, Estonia) over annexation by USSR decades earlier
- **Dec.**: Soviet leader Mikhail Gorbachev announces reduction of Soviet army

1989
- **June**: Solidarity defeat Communist candidates in free elections in Poland
- **July**: Gorbachev announces he will not oppose reform movements in Eastern Europe
- **Oct.**: Non-Communist government formed in Hungary
- **Nov.**: East Germany allows unrestricted travel to West Germany; Berlin Wall is torn down
- **Dec.**: Communist governments fall in Czechoslovakia, Bulgaria, Romania

1990
- **March**: Lithuania declares independence from Soviet Union; Soviet leader Gorbachev refuses to send troops
- **May**: U.S. and Soviet Union agree to allow reunification of Germany; Boris Yeltsin elected president of Russia
- **Oct.**: East and West Germany united into one country

1991
- **May**: Latvia and Estonia declare independence from Soviet Union
- **July**: Warsaw Pact, defensive alliance of Communist states, dissolved; U.S. and Soviet Union sign nuclear arms reduction treaty
- **Aug.**: Hard-line Communists stage coup against Gorbachev; Yeltsin leads opposition that defeats coup
- **Dec.**: Gorbachev announces dissolution of Soviet Union

60. *Place the following events in the correct order, from first to fifth. Indicate the box where each step belongs. (**Note:** On the real GED® test, you will click on each step and "drag" it into the correct box.)*

- Boris Yeltsin is elected president of Russia.
- Solidarity candidates win elections in Poland.
- Coup against Gorbachev is defeated.
- Berlin wall is torn down.
- Estonia declares independence.

First

↓

Second

↓

Third

↓

Fourth

↓

Fifth

61. Which event can most definitively be seen as the end of the Cold War?

    A. tearing down of the Berlin Wall
    B. reunification of Germany
    C. election of Solidarity government in Poland
    D. dissolution of the Soviet Union

62. *The following sentence contains blanks marked* [Select . . . ▼]*. Beneath each one is a set of choices. Indicate the choice that is correct and belongs in the blank. (**Note:** On the real GED® test, the choices will appear as a "drop-down" menu. When you click on a choice, it will appear in the blank.)*

After World War II, [Select . . . ▼] was divided into four

- Germany
- Italy
- Spain

occupation zones, one of each under the command of Britain,

France, [Select . . . ▼]

- the United States or the Soviet Union
- the United States or China
- Japan or China

Questions 63–65 are based on the following chart:

Results of World War I

Country	Outcome
Austria-Hungary	Through Treaties of Saint Germain and Trianon • Divided into separate countries: Austria, Hungary, Czechoslovakia, Yugoslavia, Romania • Also lost territory to Poland and Italy • Austria and Hungary both forced to pay reparations and reduce size of military
Britain	Gained mandates over Iraq and Palestine (modern Israel, Jordan, West Bank)
France	• Gained Alsace and Lorraine • Gained mandates over modern Syria and Lebanon from League of Nations
Germany	Through Treaty of Versailles: • Lost territory to Denmark, France, Poland • Forced to accept loosened control over some areas • Forced to pay reparations and reduce size of military
Ottoman Empire	Through Treaty of Sevres: • Lost territory in Balkans to various countries and in Southwest Asia to British and French control • Ottoman Empire overthrown, Turkish Republic established
Russia	• Experienced Communist takeover in Russian Revolution of 1917; formed Soviet Union • Lost territory in Poland through separate treaty with Germany • Invaded by Allies in attempt to restore non-Communist rule, but Soviets won
United States	• President Woodrow Wilson convinced other leaders to form League of Nations • Wilson unable to convince Senate to have U.S. join League of Nations

63. What goal did President Woodrow Wilson have that was not achieved in the peace agreements that ended World War I?

A. United States joining the League of Nations
B. success of the Russian Revolution
C. preservation of the Ottoman Empire
D. punishment of Germany for starting the war

64. Which country experienced a revolution and the establishment of a radical new regime as a result of World War I?

    A. Austria-Hungary
    B. Britain
    C. France
    D. Russia

65. Which country was *most likely* to experience unrest as a result of the harsh terms of the treaties settling World War I?

    A. Britain
    B. France
    C. Germany
    D. United States

66. The items in the following list refer either to Germany, Italy, or the Soviet Union during the 1930s and World War II. *Indicate the box where each item belongs. (**Note:** On the real GED® test, you will click on each item and "drag" it into the correct box.)*

Fascism	U.S. ally in WWII	Stalin
Hitler	Communism	Mussolini
Holocaust	invaded Ethiopia	invaded Soviet Union
Nazism		

Germany	Italy

Soviet Union

67. *The following sentence contains a blank marked* Select... ▼. *Beneath it is a set of choices. Indicate the choice that is correct and belongs in the blank. (**Note:** On the real GED® test, the choices will appear as a "drop-down" menu. When you click on a choice, it will appear in the blank.)*

Nazi Germany and Stalin's Soviet Union are considered Select... ▼

- totalitarian
- democratic
- capitalist

states because the government exercised complete control over society.

68. What was the purpose of the GI Bill passed during World War II?

A. to encourage more enlistments
B. to desegregate the armed forces
C. to provide veterans with educational and housing aid
D. to institute a draft calling for mandatory service

Question 69 is based on the following map:

The Trail of Tears

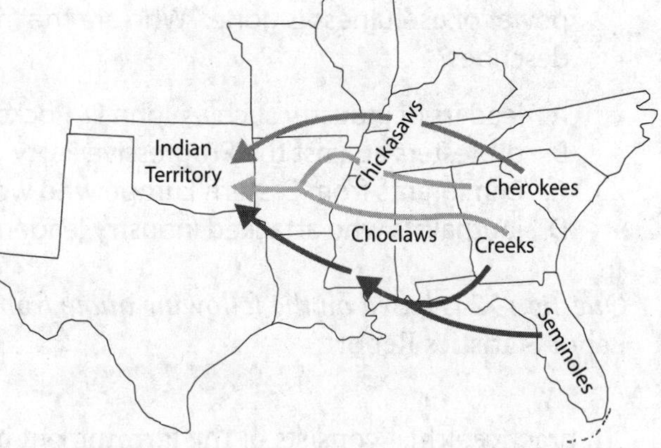

69. The map represents what policy pursued by the U.S. government?

    A. advance of Union army in the Civil War
    B. forced removal of Native Americans from traditional lands
    C. westward expansion at the expense of Mexico
    D. seizure of Louisiana Territory

Question 70 is based on the following map:

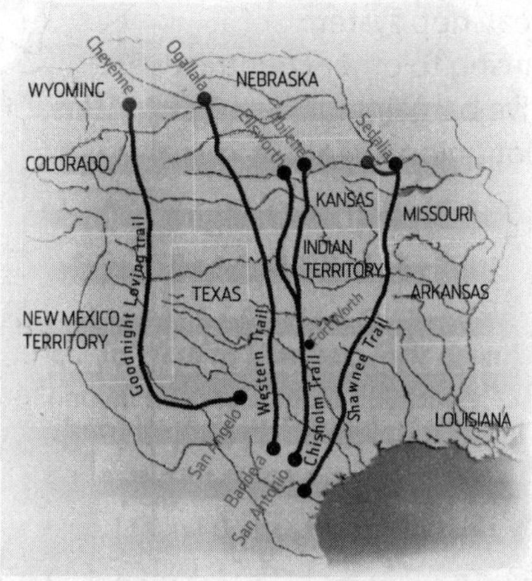

Source: https://tpwd.texas.gov/education/resources/keep-texas-wild/vaqueros-and-cowboys/images-1/spike_answer_map.jpg.

70. Based on the map, which state was most involved in the cattle business? *Write your answer on the blank.*

    ____

71. Teddy Roosevelt said, "Men with the muckrake are often indispensable to the well-being of society, but only if they know when to stop raking the muck, and to look upward to the celestial crown above them . . . If they gradually grow to feel that the whole world is nothing but muck, their power of usefulness is gone." Who are the "men with the muckrake" he describes?

    A. leaders of industry such as John D. Rockefeller
    B. protesters against the Progressive Party
    C. immigrants from Eastern Europe who worked in factories
    D. journalists who attacked industry leaders and institutions as corrupt

Question 72 is based on the following quote from the 1893 Illinois Bureau of Labor Statistics Report:

"In practice, [this] consists of the farming out by competing manufacturers to competing contractors the material for garments, which, in turn, is distributed among competing men and women to be made up. The middleman, or contractor, is the [oppressor] (though he also may be himself subjected to pressure from above) and his employees are the . . . oppressed. He contracts to make up certain garments, at a given price per piece, and then hires other people to do the work at a less price. His profit lies in the difference between the two prices."

72. Which of the following systems does the passage above describe?

    A. the sweatshop system
    B. outsourcing to other countries
    C. collective bargaining
    D. the labor union system

Question 73 is based on the following map:

The United States in 1810

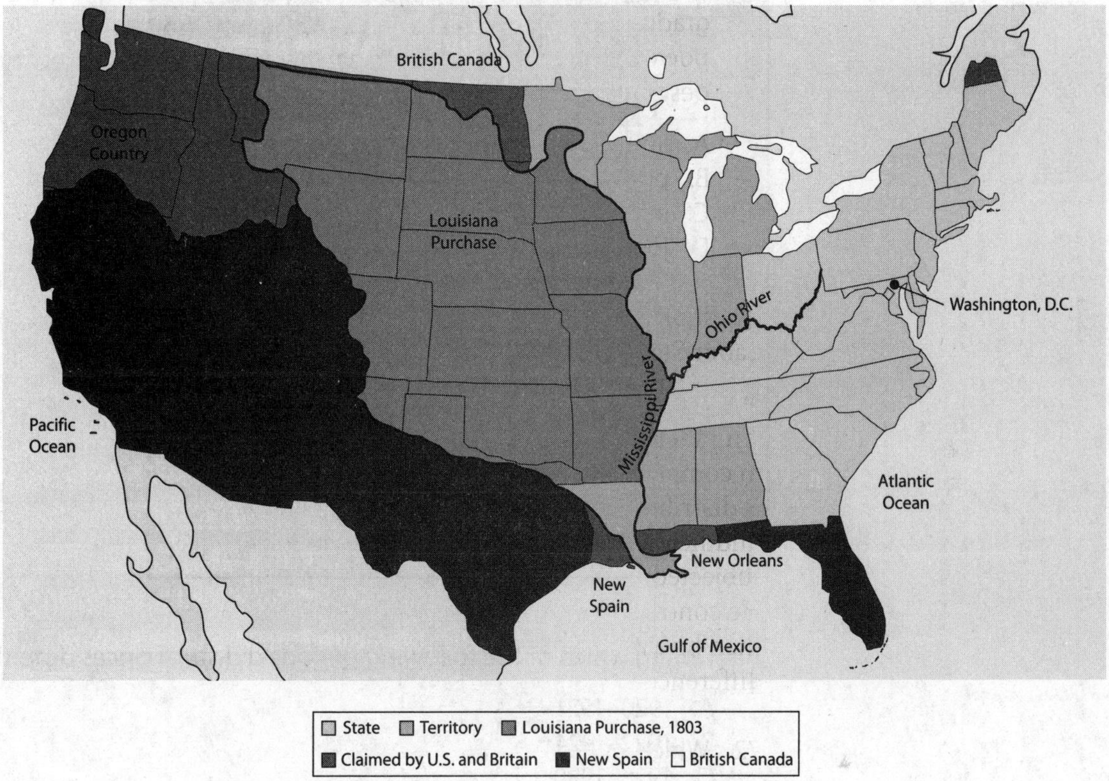

73. Which conclusion can be drawn from the map?

    A. The territory of the Louisiana Purchase originally belonged to Spain.
    B. The western boundary of the Louisiana Purchase is the Colorado River.
    C. The Louisiana Purchase nearly doubled the size of the United States.
    D. The legality of the Louisiana Purchase was disputed by Spain.

Question 74 is based on the following chart:

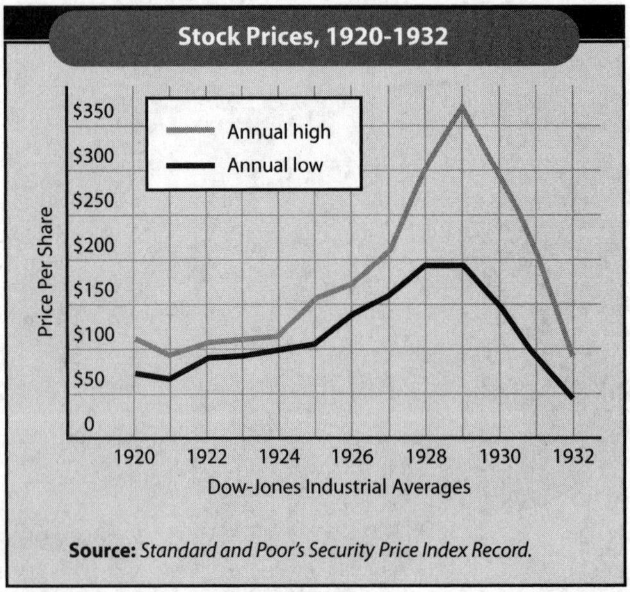

74. During which of the following periods did stock prices drop the most?

 A. 1920–1921
 B. 1922–1924
 C. 1928–1930
 D. 1930–1932

Question 75 is based on the following map:

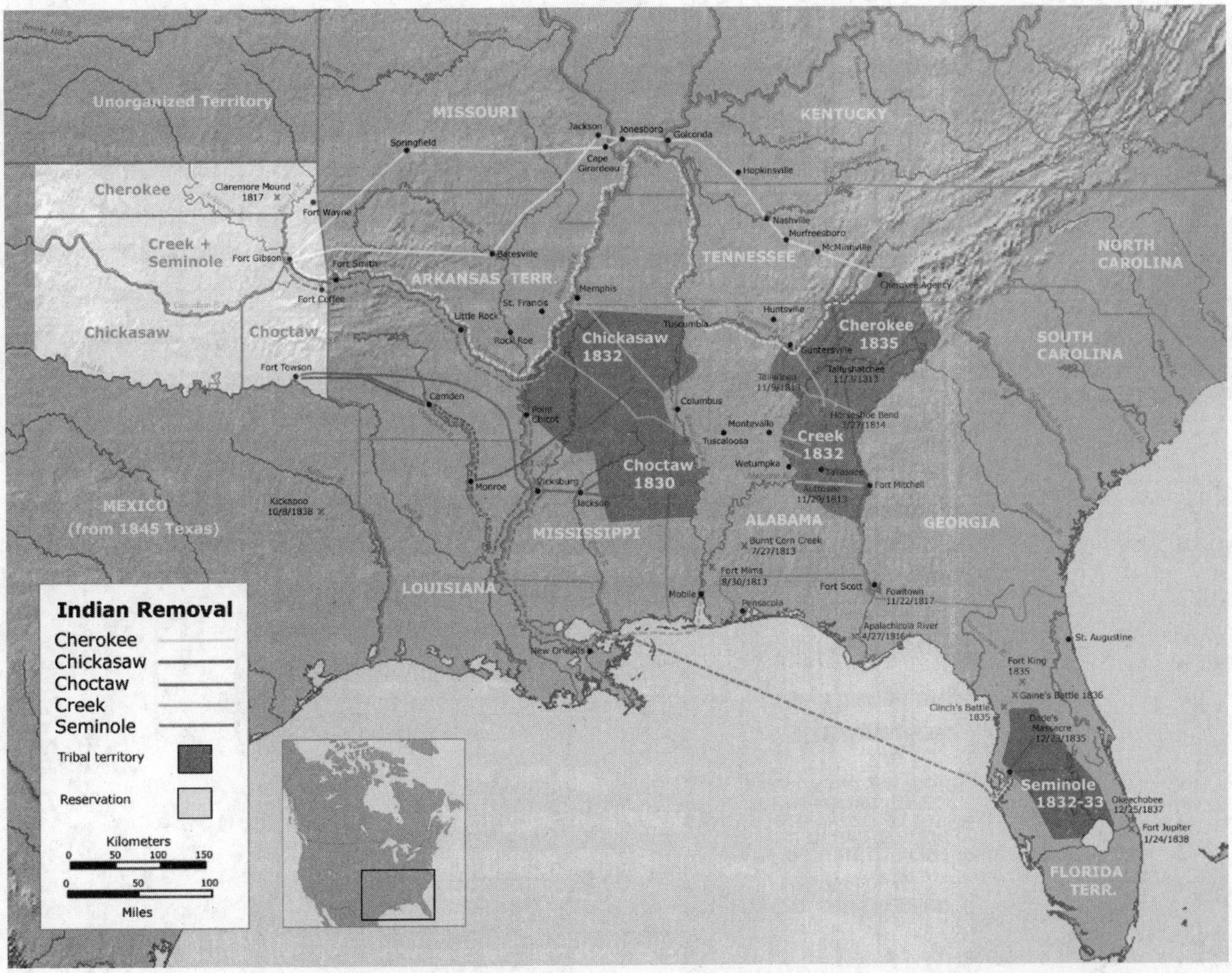

Source: Background map courtesy of Demis, www.demis.nl and Wilcomb E. Washburn (Hrsg.) *Handbook of North American Indians, Vol. 4: History of Indian–White Relations*. Smithsonian Institution Press, Washington DC, 1988. ISBN 0-16004-583-5, Public Domain, https://commons.wikimedia.org/w/index.php?curid=2681249.

75. What conclusion can be drawn from the map?

  A. No further lands in Florida were taken after 1833.
  B. The Cherokee, Choctaw, Chickasaw, Seminole, and Creek tribes were the only ones to lose their native lands.
  C. The general trend shows U.S. seizure of native lands moving westward.
  D. The Chickasaw tribe's native lands were all in what is now Mississippi.

THIS IS THE END OF CHAPTER 2: U.S. HISTORY.

CHAPTER 3

Economics

Directions: Answer the following questions. For multiple-choice questions, choose the best answer. For other questions, follow the directions preceding the question. Answers begin on page 178.

1. Which of the following constitutes a market?

   A. a public park
   B. a toll road
   C. a sidewalk
   D. a family gathering

*Questions 2–4 are based on the following illustration. (**Note**: On the real GED® test, you will click on the illustration you want to indicate.)*

Donna: hourly wage plus productivity bonus

Julian: part-time, low hourly wage plus tips

Gerald: full-time, weekly salary

Marina: commission

2. *Indicate the worker whose income is not based on the number of hours worked.*

    ____

3. *Indicate the worker whose total income includes a guaranteed base salary plus incentives based on output.*

    ____

4. *Indicate the worker who earns a set amount regardless of how hard he or she works.*

    ____

Questions 5–7 are based on the following pie charts:

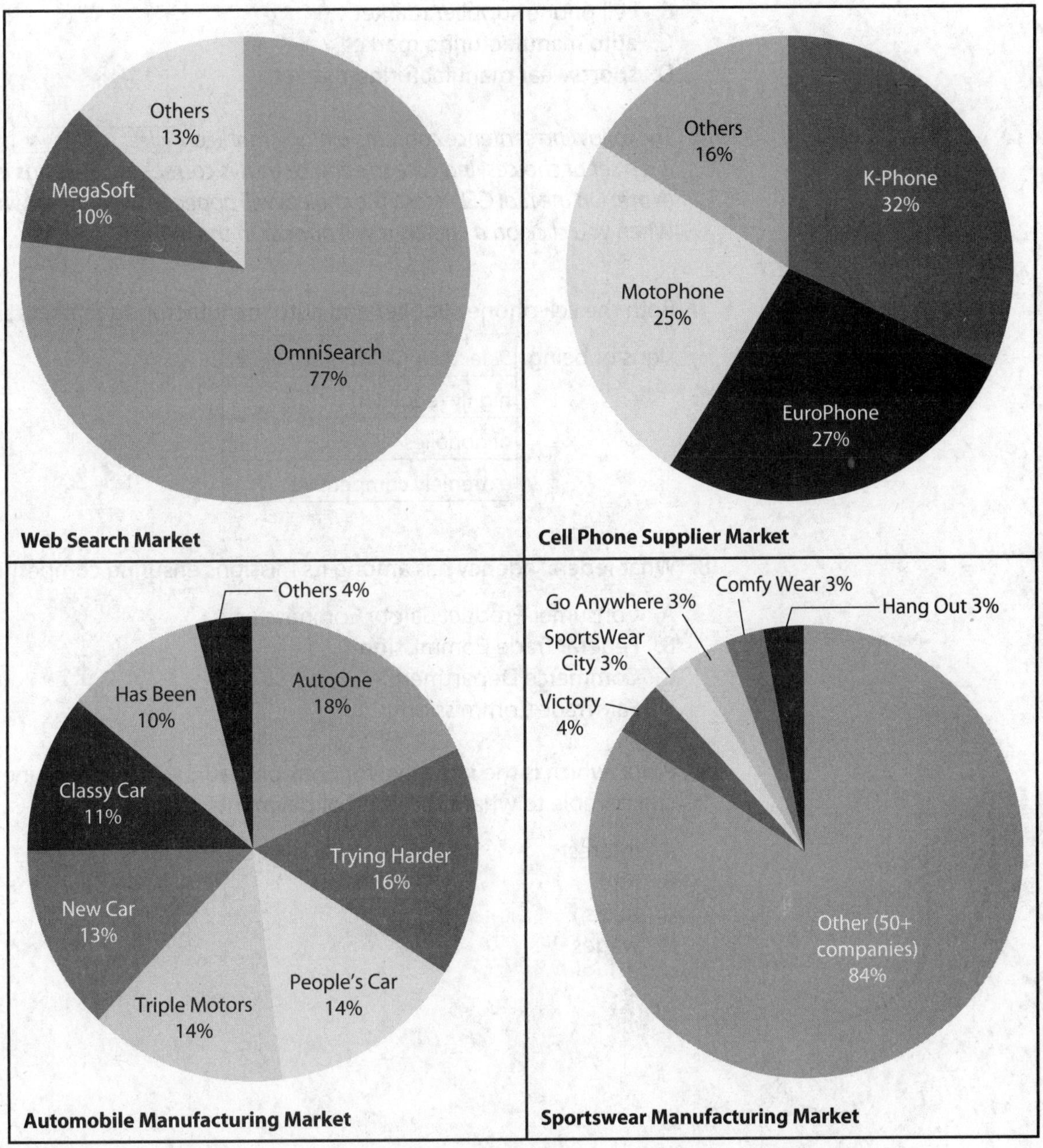

5. Which market is the closest to having free competition?

   A. web search market
   B. cell phone supplier market
   C. auto manufacturing market
   D. sportswear manufacturing market

6. Which market comes closest to having monopolistic market conditions?

   A. web search market
   B. cell phone supplier market
   C. auto manufacturing market
   D. sportswear manufacturing market

7. *The following sentence contains a blank marked* Select... ▼. *Beneath it is a set of choices. Indicate the choice that is correct and belongs in the blank. (**Note:** On the real GED® test, the choices will appear as a "drop-down" menu. When you click on a choice, it will appear in the blank.)*

   Both the cell phone supplier and auto manufacturing markets show signs of being Select... ▼ .

Select... ▼
highly regulated
oligopolies
extremely competitive

8. What federal agency has among its missions ensuring competition?

   A. Consumer Product Safety Commission
   B. Federal Trade Commission
   C. Commerce Department
   D. Fair Trade Commission

9. Profit, which is the incentive for entrepreneurs to open a business, is comparable to what other kind of payment?

   A. interest
   B. rent
   C. taxes
   D. wages

Questions 10–13 are based on the following graph of supply and demand:

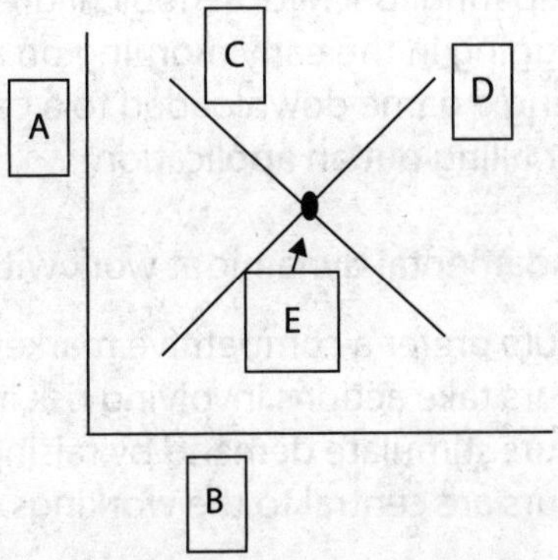

10. What label should be placed at location A?

    A. Demand
    B. Price
    C. Quantity
    D. Supply

11. What label should be placed at location B?

    A. Demand
    B. Price
    C. Quantity
    D. Supply

12. What label should be placed at location D?

    A. Demand
    B. Price
    C. Quantity
    D. Supply

13. *The following sentence contains a blank marked* Select... ▼. *Beneath it is a set of choices. Indicate the choice that is correct and belongs in the blank. (**Note:** On the real GED® test, the choices will appear as a "drop-down" menu. When you click on a choice, it will appear in the blank.)*

    Location E in this graph indicates the Select... ▼

Select... ▼
quantity demanded
quantity supplied
equilibrium price

14. Which of the following activities takes place in a market?

   A. a parent preparing lunch for schoolchildren
   B. a person jogging in the early morning on a city street
   C. a teen playing a game downloaded to a cell phone months before
   D. a job seeker filling out an application

15. What is the fundamental dynamic at work with entrepreneurship?

   A. Entrepreneurs prefer a competitive marketplace.
   B. Entrepreneurs take actions involving risk in the hope of making profits.
   C. Entrepreneurs stimulate demand by raising prices.
   D. Entrepreneurs are central to the workings of a command economy.

16. What kind of tax are tariffs most similar to?

   A. income tax
   B. property tax
   C. reduced tax
   D. sales tax

*Questions 17–18 are based on the following illustrations. (**Note:** On the real GED® test, you will click on the illustration you want to indicate.)*

Factor 1

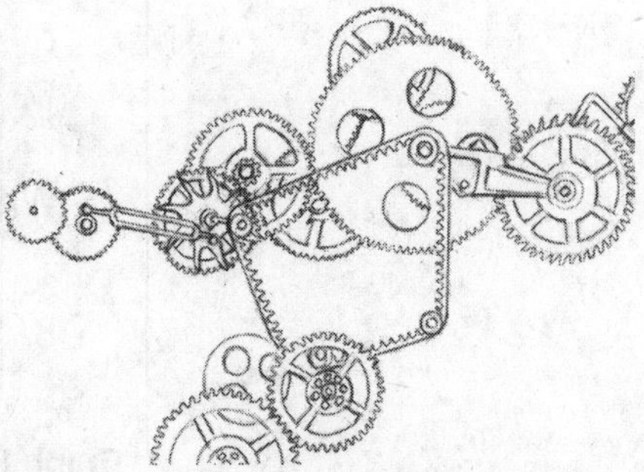

Factor 2

Factor 3

Factor 4

17. *Indicate the drawing that represents the factor of production of physical capital.*

    ____

18. *Indicate the drawing that represents the factor of production of labor.*

    ____

19. The Sherman and Clayton Antitrust Acts have the goal of addressing what market failure?

    A. causing pollution
    B. union organizing
    C. inability to provide public goods
    D. lack of competition

*Questions 20–22 are based on the following graphs. (**Note**: On the real GED® test, you will click on the box you want to indicate.)*

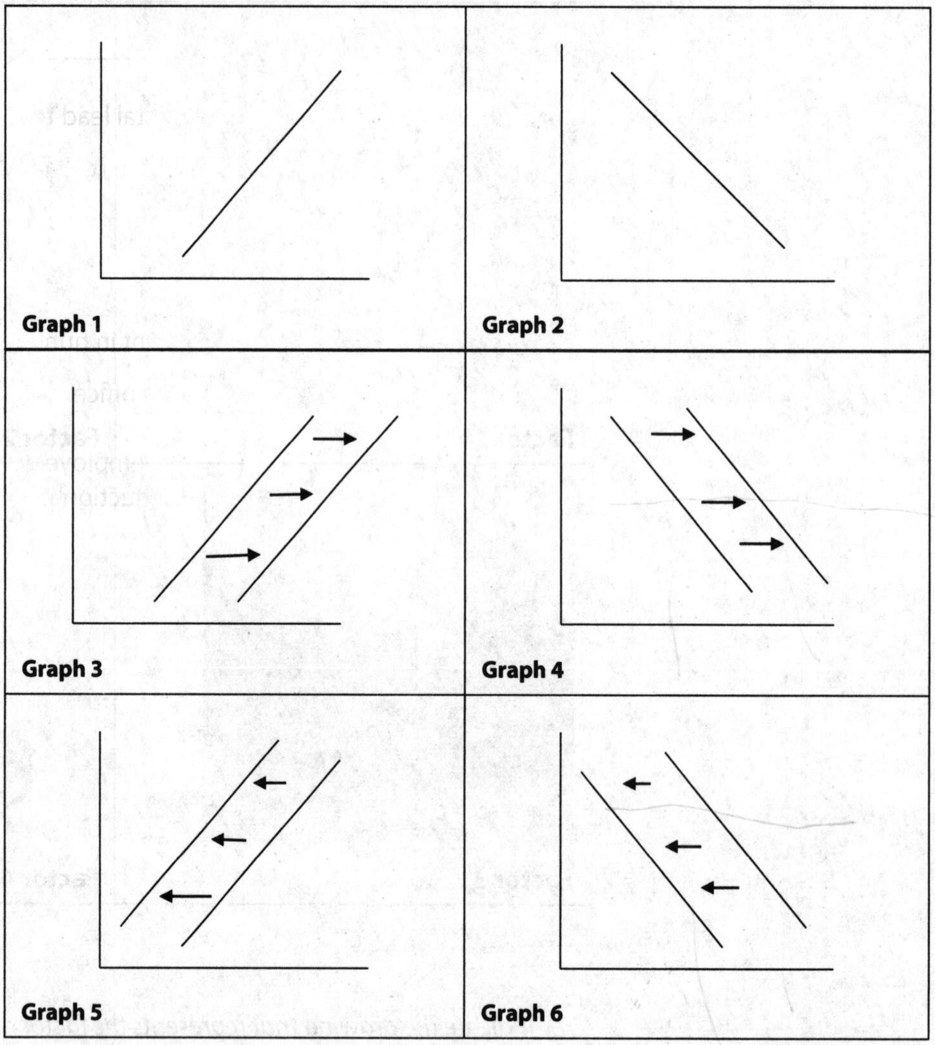

20. *Indicate the graph that shows a basic supply curve.*

    ____

21. *Indicate the graph that shows a supply curve showing the effects of new technology that allows for more efficient production.*

    ____

22. *Indicate the graph that shows a demand curve showing the effects of new technology that results in a substitute product that is cheaper than the original product.*

    ____

23. How does the investment of capital lead to economic growth?

    A. by increasing demand
    B. by increasing specialization
    C. by reducing opportunity cost
    D. by increasing productivity

24. Which is an example of investment in human capital?

    A. buying new computers for an office
    B. building new housing
    C. providing training classes for employees
    D. instituting more efficient production processes

Questions 25–26 are based on the following diagram of the fundamental problem addressed by economics:

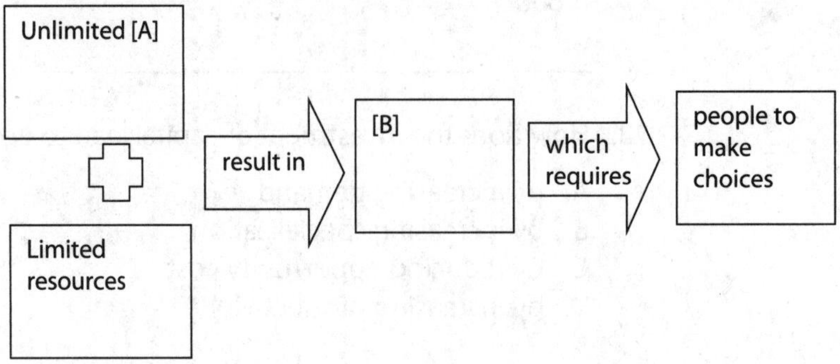

25. What economic term belongs in space [A] in this diagram?

    A. factors
    B. hopes
    C. capital
    D. wants

26. What term belongs in space [B]?

    A. dilemmas
    B. opportunity cost
    C. risk
    D. scarcity

27. *The following sentence contains a blank marked* Select... ▼. *Beneath it is a set of choices. Indicate the choice that is correct and belongs in the blank. (**Note:** On the real GED® test, the choices will appear as a "drop-down" menu. When you click on a choice, it will appear in the blank.)*

    An auto loan is the type of credit called Select... ▼

    - installment credit
    - open credit
    - revolving credit

    in which the borrower pays a set amount each month until the loan is paid off.

28. In a loan or credit agreement, why might finance charges be more than the interest on the loan?

    A. They also include taxes.
    B. They include compound interest.
    C. They include any fees as well as interest.
    D. They include the principal.

*Questions 29–30 are based on the following graphs. (**Note**: On the real GED® test, you will click on the box you want to indicate.)*

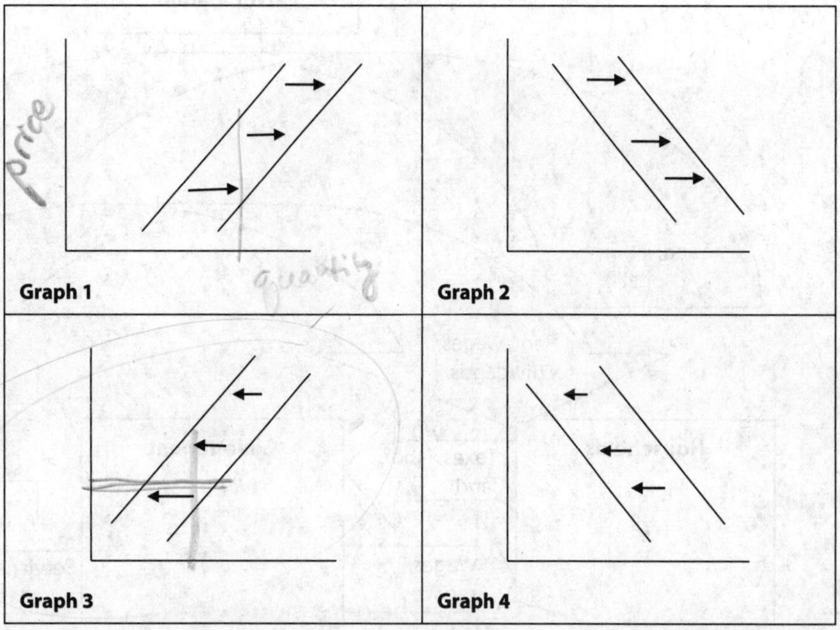

29. *Indicate the graph that shows the effect on domestic supply of lowering tariffs when foreign suppliers can produce a good at a lower cost than domestic producers.*

____

30. *Indicate the graph that shows the effect on domestic demand of lowering tariffs when foreign suppliers can produce a good at a lower cost than domestic producers.*

____

31. Which of the following markets is likely to be the most competitive because of ease of entry?

    A. laboratory services
    B. dry cleaners
    C. car dealerships
    D. supermarkets

32. What is the law of supply?

    A. Supply always exceeds demand.
    B. Supply is always less than demand because of scarcity.
    C. Supply increases as price increases.
    D. Supply decreases as price increases.

Questions 33–35 are based on the following diagram:

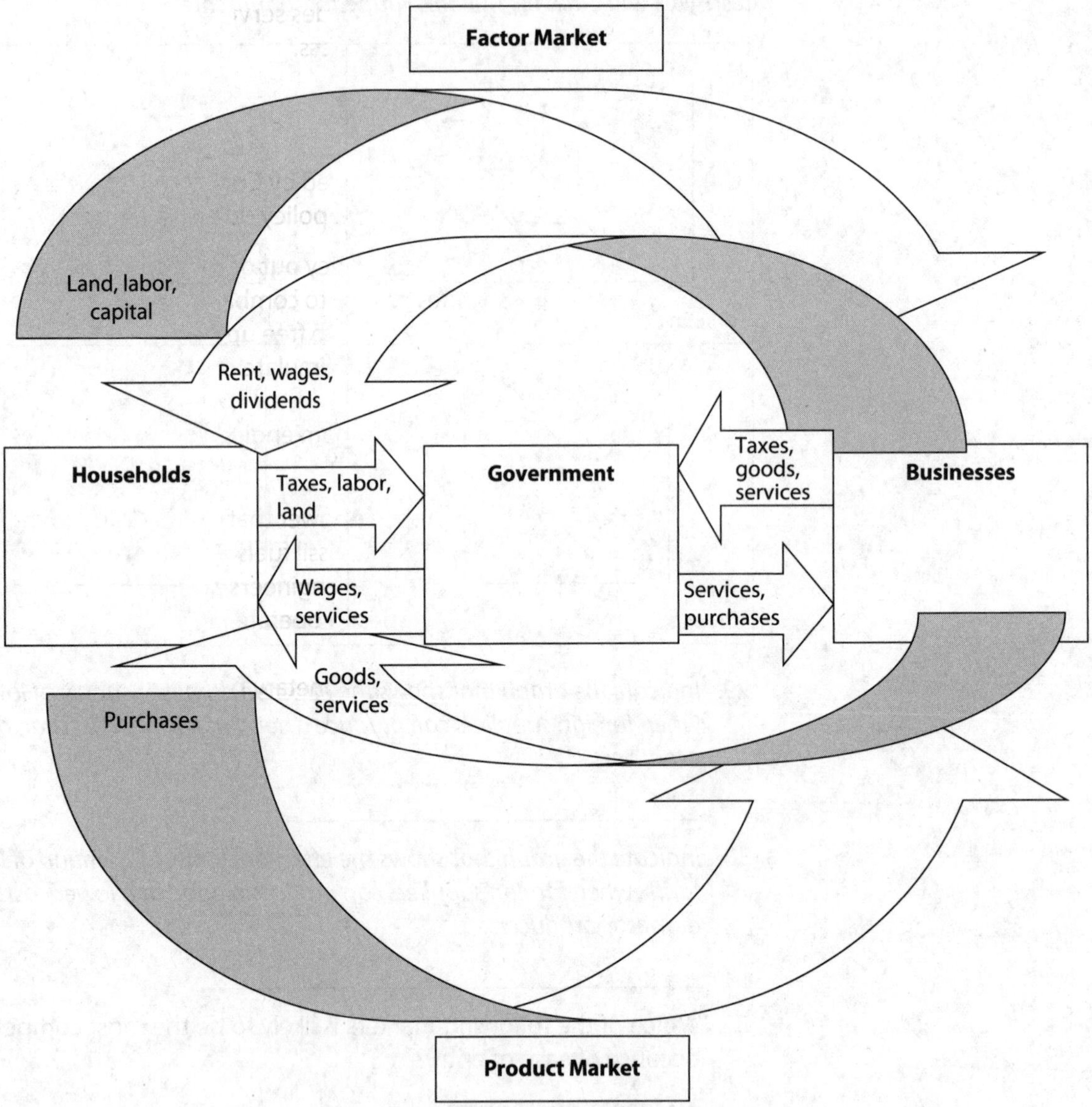

33. This diagram illustrates what fundamental economic concept?
    A. laws of supply and demand
    B. circular flow of goods and services
    C. law of diminishing returns
    D. business cycle

34. According to this diagram, who owns the factors of production?
    A. businesses
    B. government
    C. households
    D. households and businesses

35. How is the role of the government similar to that of business?

    A. It purchases factors and provides services.
    B. It provides a market for business.
    C. It collects taxes.
    D. It is composed of households.

36. The American Recovery Act, passed by Congress in 2009, was an example of what government use of fiscal policy during a recession?

    A. increasing taxes to draw money out of the economy
    B. tightening the money supply to combat inflation
    C. loosening the money supply to free up credit
    D. boosting spending to try to stimulate demand

37. Why was the invention of the steam engine so important to the Industrial Revolution?

    A. It provided a new source of power that increased output.
    B. It replaced more expensive fossil fuels as a source of power.
    C. It led to increased wages for engineers and mechanics.
    D. It allowed the first factories to operate.

38. What institution oversees U.S. monetary policy and ensures that the banking system is sound?

    A. Comptroller of the Currency
    B. Department of the Treasury
    C. Federal Reserve Board
    D. U.S. Mint

Questions 39–41 are based on the following chart:

Economic Systems		
System	**Characteristic**	**Benefits and Drawbacks**
Traditional	Answers basic economic questions by following past patterns	Little freedom of choice Meets basic needs of society, but for limited population Uses resources fairly efficiently Low productivity Little innovation Little variety of goods and services
Market	Individuals and businesses answer the basic economic questions by acting on self-interest	High freedom of choice Opportunity of reward, but with risk High productivity High innovation Great variety of goods and services High-quality goods and services Little protection from market failures, such as monopoly, unfair practices, pollution, business cycle
Command	Government answers the basic economic questions	Low freedom of choice Low productivity Low innovation Relatively low variety of goods and services Relatively low quality of goods and services High level of security through guaranteed employment, social services
Mixed	Individuals answer the basic economic questions by acting on self-interest, but government plays a role to address market failures	Benefits of market economy but at slightly reduced levels (e.g., less freedom of choice) Reduced risks of market economy Cost of government

39. Which of the following is a benefit of a traditional economy?

A. It is suitable only for a limited population.
B. It uses resources fairly efficiently.
C. Productivity is low.
D. There is little innovation.

40. Which economic system has low productivity and efficiency because of the lack of incentives and freedom?

    A. traditional
    B. market
    C. command
    D. mixed

41. What economic system does the United States have?

    A. traditional
    B. market
    C. command
    D. mixed

Question 42 is based on the following illustration:

Drawing 1

Drawing 2

Drawing 3

Drawing 4

42. Which drawing represents the kind of market failure called an *externality,* which is a cost imposed on others by one economic actor's behavior? *Write the correct drawing number in the blank.*

    ____

43. What is an example of the government's role in meeting market failures in a mixed economy?

    A. operation of the stock market
    B. workplace health and safety laws
    C. corporate research and development spending
    D. nonprofit organizations providing community services

44. In terms of its market area, a professional sports team has what kind of market position?

    A. free competition
    B. oligopoly
    C. monopoly
    D. regulated utility

45. In terms of the entertainment market, a professional sports team has what kind of market position?

    A. free competition
    B. oligopoly
    C. monopoly
    D. regulated utility

Questions 46–47 are based on the following diagram:

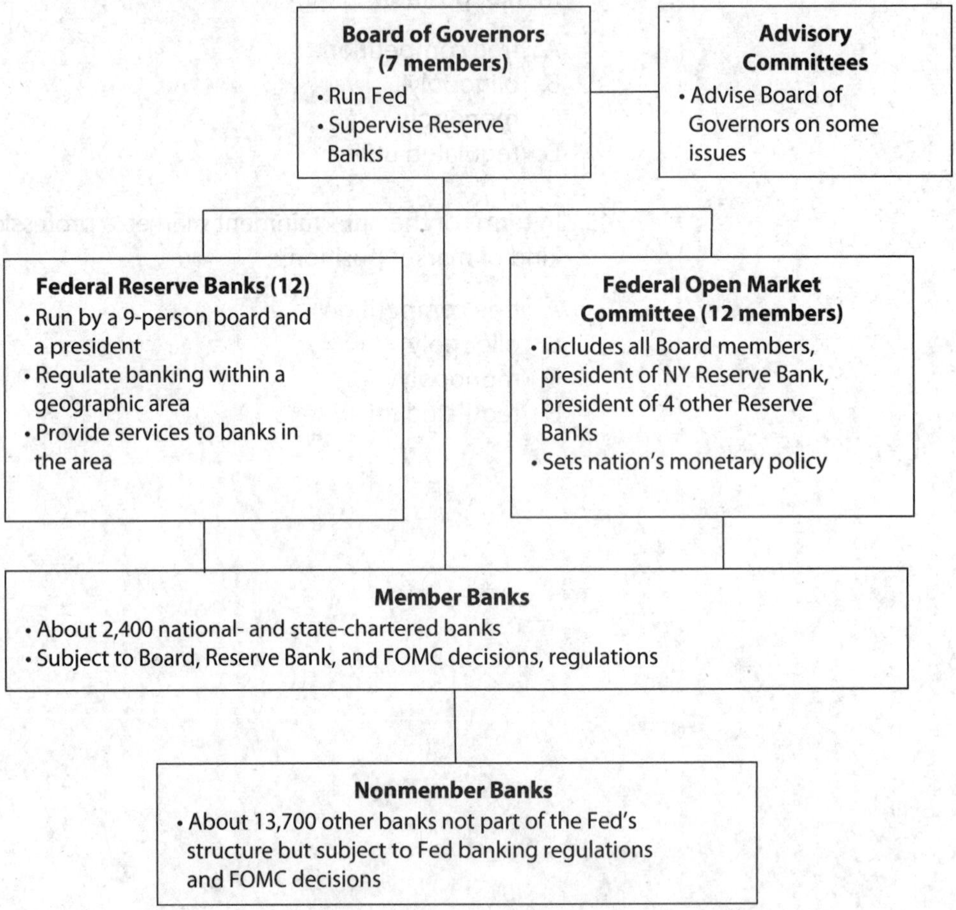

46. Which body sets national monetary policy?

    A. Board of Governors
    B. Federal Open Market Committee
    C. Federal Reserve Banks
    D. member banks

47. How does the Federal Reserve System affect banking in the United States in general?

    A. by requiring membership in the system
    B. by implementing the president's monetary policy
    C. through taxation
    D. through banking regulations

Questions 48–49 are based on the following quotation:

"England may be so circumstanced, that to produce the cloth may require the labor of 100 men for one year; and if she attempted to make the wine, it might require the labor of 120 men for the same time. England would therefore find it in her interest to import wine, and to purchase it by the exportation of cloth.

To produce the wine in Portugal, might require only the labor of 80 men for one year, and to produce the cloth in the same country, might require the labor of 90 men for the same time. It would therefore be advantageous for her to export wine in exchange for cloth . . . notwithstanding that the commodity imported by Portugal could be produced there with less labor than in England."

—David Ricardo, *On the Principles of Political Economy, and Taxation*
Source: from Project Gutenberg.

48. Based on this analysis, Ricardo recommends that England concentrate on producing wool, which illustrates what economic concept?

    A. comparative advantage
    B. laissez-faire
    C. mercantilism
    D. supply and demand

49. Following Ricardo's reasoning leads nations to focus on producing the goods and services at which they are most efficient, a practice called

    A. absolute advantage
    B. productivity
    C. specialization
    D. investment

Questions 50–52 are based on the following passage:

The United States Congress has enacted several key consumer protection laws. The Equal Credit Opportunity Act bans discrimination in credit decisions based on various demographic factors (age, race, gender) or because a consumer's income comes from public assistance. The Fair Credit Billing Act establishes procedures to follow in a credit billing dispute. The Fair Credit Reporting Act requires creditors to inform consumers of the agency issuing a credit report on which credit was denied, gives consumers access to their credit report, and establishes a procedure for disputing information in a credit report. The Fair Debt Collections Practices Act sets rules for individuals and businesses contacting consumers about unpaid debts. The Truth in Lending Act sets the information that lenders must disclose to borrowers to clarify the terms of a credit transaction prior to completion of the agreement.

50. Which law *most likely* contains the provision that requires lenders to notify potential borrowers of the interest rate, finance charges, and annual percentage rate (APR) of a loan?

    A. Equal Credit Opportunity Act
    B. Fair Credit Billing Act
    C. Fair Credit Reporting Act
    D. Truth in Lending Act

51. A consumer who receives Social Security payments and is denied credit could try to protest the decision based on what law?

    A. Equal Credit Opportunity Act
    B. Fair Credit Billing Act
    C. Fair Credit Reporting Act
    D. Fair Debt Collections Practices Act

52. Consumer credit laws are examples of government intervention in the economy as a result of addressing what goal?

    A. competition
    B. fair trade
    C. market failures
    D. public goods

53. Which of the following defines the economic concept of *opportunity cost*?

   A. the disappointment experienced as a result of missing a valuable opportunity
   B. the next most attractive alternative, given up when making an economic choice
   C. the risks associated with any opportunity for a potential economic reward
   D. the analysis of the costs and benefits of any economic decision

Questions 54–55 are based on the following graph:

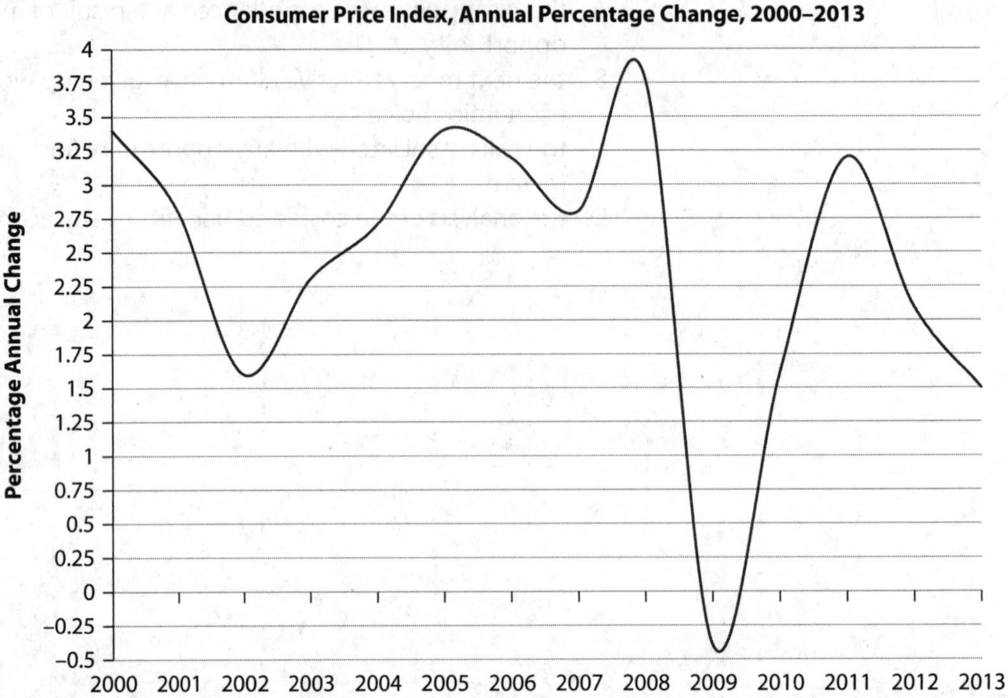

Source: Bureau of Labor Statistics.

54. In which year did prices rise most sharply? *Write your answer in the blank.*

____

55. Based on the data shown in the graph, a recession (a kind of economic downturn) was *most likely* to have begun in which year? *Write your answer in the blank.*

____

56. The government collects the data that forms the Consumer Price Index (CPI) in order to track what economic problem?

    A. growth
    B. inflation
    C. productivity
    D. unemployment

Questions 57–58 are based on the following graph:

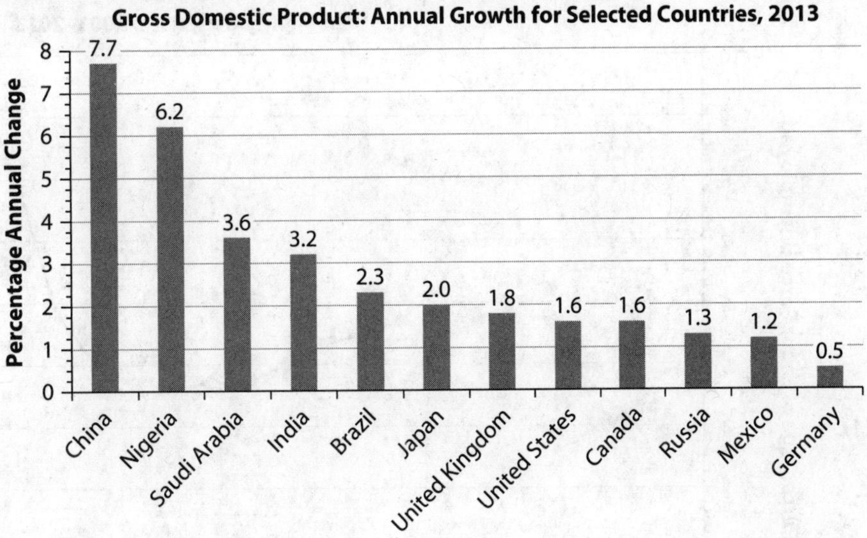

Source: CIA World Factbook 2014.

57. Compared to the United States, China's economy grew approximately how much faster in 2013?

    A. about two times
    B. nearly five times
    C. almost eight times
    D. nearly ten times

58. What generalization can reasonably be made on the basis of these data?

    A. Older industrialized economies performed less well than newly industrialized economies.
    B. European economies were outperforming those of other regions.
    C. Growth was lowest in Africa.
    D. Despite its problems, the United States was growing substantially.

Questions 59–60 are based on the following graph:

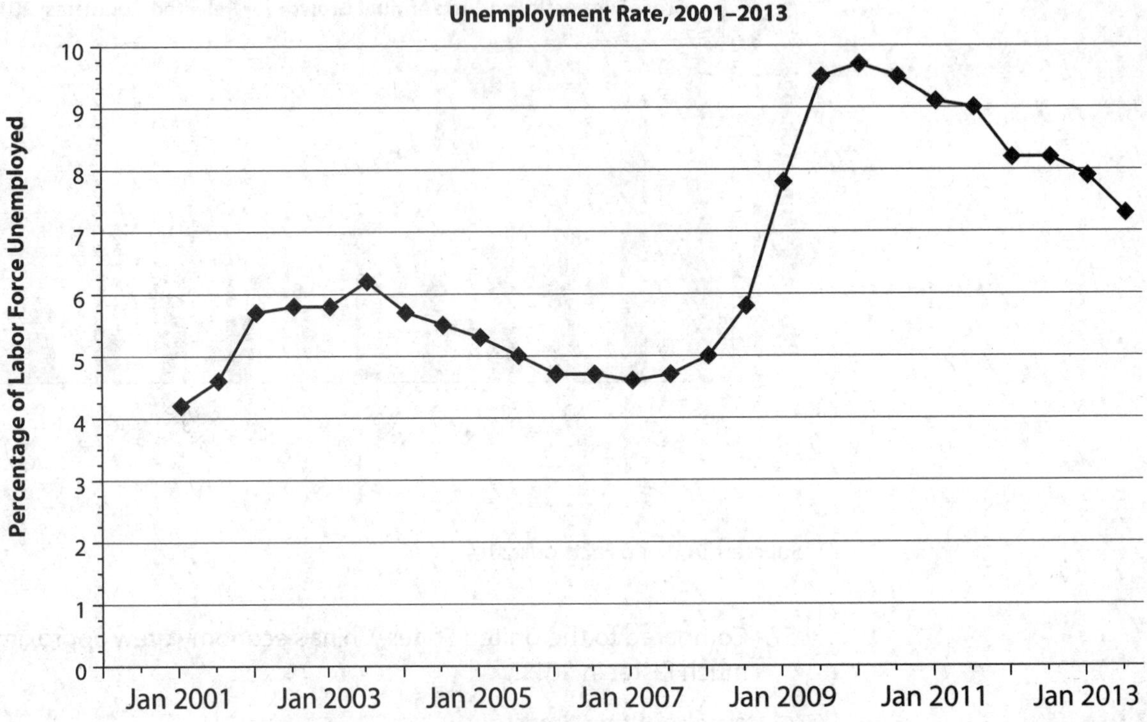

Source: Bureau of Labor Statistics, U.S. Dept. of Labor.

59. In the period covered by the graph, the unemployment rate was lowest in early 2001. In later years, when did the rate again approach that low level?

    A. late 2002–early 2003
    B. late 2006–early 2007
    C. late 2008–early 2009
    D. late 2010–early 2013

60. The federal government may use fiscal policy to try to stimulate the economy in a period of high and rising unemployment. In which period shown on this graph would such an action have been most likely?

    A. early 2004
    B. late 2005–early 2006
    C. early 2009
    D. late 2012–early 2013

Questions 61–62 are based on the following chart:

	Chief Exports	**Chief Imports**
European Union	machinery, motor vehicles, pharmaceuticals and other chemicals, fuels, aircraft, plastics, iron and steel, wood pulp and paper products, alcoholic beverages, furniture	fuels and crude oil, machinery, vehicles, pharmaceuticals and other chemicals, precious gemstones, textiles, aircraft, plastics, metals, ships
China	electrical and other machinery, including data processing equipment, apparel, radio telephone handsets, textiles, integrated circuits	electrical and other machinery; oil and mineral fuels; nuclear reactor, boiler, and machinery components; optical and medical equipment; metal ores; motor vehicles; soybeans
Japan	motor vehicles, semiconductors, iron and steel products, auto parts, plastic materials, power-generating machinery	petroleum, liquid natural gas, clothing, semiconductors, coal, audio and visual apparatus
United States	agricultural products (soybeans, fruit, corn), industrial supplies (organic chemicals), capital goods (transistors, aircraft, motor vehicle parts, computers, telecommunications equipment), consumer goods (automobiles, medicines)	agricultural products, industrial supplies (including crude oil), capital goods (computers, telecommunications equipment, motor vehicle parts, office machines, electric power machinery), consumer goods (automobiles, clothing, medicines, furniture, toys)

Source: CIA World Factbook.

61. What economic principles are demonstrated by these imports and exports?

A. power of incentives to spur entrepreneurship
B. global reach of multinationals
C. benefits of free trade agreements
D. specialization leading to interdependence

62. What can be inferred about Japan from the list of Japanese exports and imports?

A. lack of an agricultural base
B. lack of energy resources
C. development of a postindustrial economy
D. relatively weak manufacturing base

Question 63 is based on the following passage:

"People are classified as unemployed if they do not have a job, have actively looked for work in the prior 4 weeks, and are currently available for work. Actively looking for work may consist of any of the following activities:

- Contacting:
  - — An employer directly or having a job interview
  - — A public or private employment agency
  - — Friends or relatives
  - — A school or university employment center
- Submitting resumes or filling out applications
- Placing or answering job advertisements
- Checking union or professional registers
- Some other means of active job search

Passive methods of job search do not have the potential to connect job seekers with potential employers and therefore do not qualify as active job search methods. Examples of passive methods include attending a job training program or course, or merely reading about job openings that are posted in newspapers or on the Internet."

—Bureau of Labor Statistics, "How the Government Measures Unemployment"

63. One criticism of government unemployment statistics is that they do not count which group of individuals?

A. people who are unemployed but have given up on finding work
B. spouses who have not entered the workforce
C. people who are part-time students at a college or university
D. people who lose their jobs due to outsourcing

Questions 64–66 are based on the following diagram:

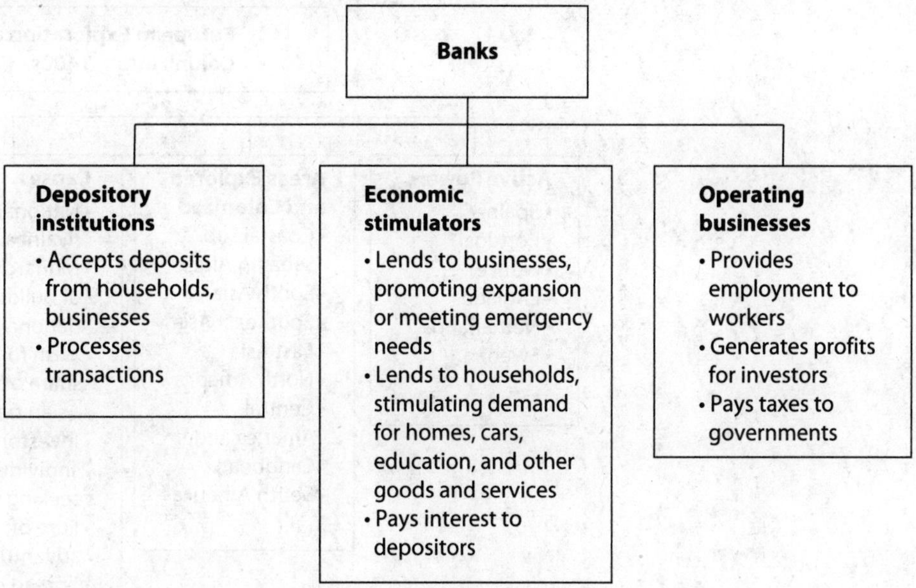

64. What is an appropriate title for this diagram?
    - A. The Roles of Banks
    - B. The Costs and Benefits of Banking
    - C. Regulation of the Banking System
    - D. Changes in American Banking

65. Why do banks pay interest to depositors?
    - A. to meet federal requirements
    - B. to satisfy shareholders
    - C. as incentives to depositors
    - D. to generate income for lending

66. In which role do banks increase the money supply through the multiplier effect?
    - A. as businesses
    - B. as depository institutions
    - C. as employers
    - D. as lenders

Question 67 is based on the following diagram:

European Exploration and Colonization, 1400s–1700s

Active Powers
- Spain
- Portugal
- France
- England
- Netherlands
- Sweden

Areas Explored and Colonized
- Coastal sub-Saharan Africa
- South Asia
- Southeast Asia
- East Asia
- North America
- Central America and Caribbean
- South America

Causes
- Nationalist rivalries
- Monarchs' goal of building national treasuries
- Wish for greater share of Asian trade
- Investors and individuals seeking wealth
- Lure of adventure
- Spread of Christianity

Effects
- Creation of new colonial empires
- Increased monarchical power
- Promotion of capitalism
- European settlement of Americas
- Collapse of Native American empires and population
- Development of Atlantic slave trade

67. What was an economic cause of the era of European exploration and colonization of the fifteenth to eighteenth centuries?

A. desire to promote capitalism
B. wish for greater share of Asian trade
C. desire to profit from the slave trade
D. monarchs' and individuals' desire for power

Questions 68–69 are based on the following chart:

Type of Account or Investment	Risk	Reward
Savings account	Low (insured, with limits, by FDIC* so principal cannot be lost)	Low
Bank money market accounts	Low (insured, with limits, by FDIC so principal cannot be lost)	Relatively low
Money market mutual funds	Relatively low (not insured but generally stable in value)	Relatively low
Municipal bonds	Moderate (issuer may default)	Moderate
Federal bonds	Fairly low (U.S. government unlikely to default)	Moderate
Corporate bonds	Moderate (issuer may default)	Moderate to high
Stocks	Very high: can lose investment	Potentially very high when sold; can also receive dividends during time stock is held

*FDIC = Federal Deposit Insurance Corporation

68. Why are savings and money market accounts in banks the most secure method of saving or investing?
    A. Banks are careful with money.
    B. Those accounts carry the highest reward.
    C. Banks guarantee to keep enough to pay all deposits on demand.
    D. The principal cannot be lost because the accounts are insured.

69. What generalization can be made about investing?
    A. The higher the risk, the greater the potential reward.
    B. Bonds are safer than money market accounts.
    C. Stocks are not worth investing in because of the risk of losing capital.
    D. Savings accounts are worthless because of the low reward.

Questions 70–71 are based on the following diagram:

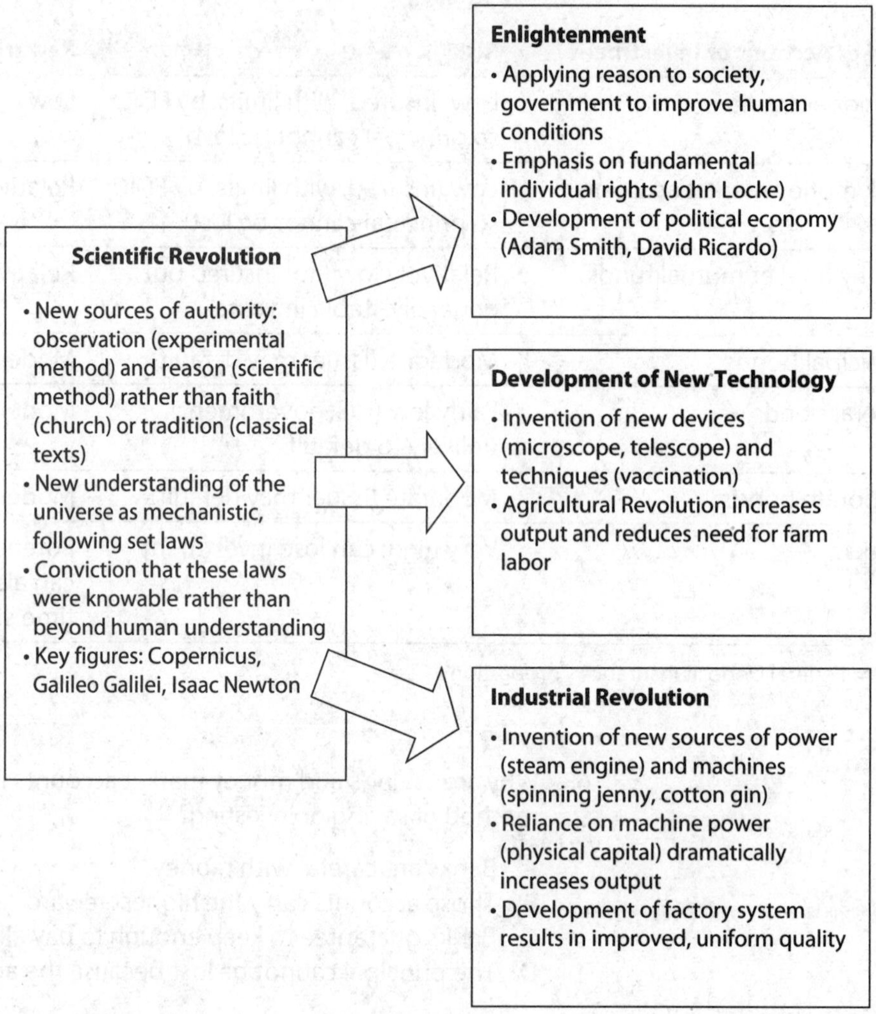

70. How did the Scientific Revolution help bring about the Industrial Revolution?
    A. The loosening of church authority weakened opposition to industrialization.
    B. The perception of the universe as mechanistic and knowable prompted inventions.
    C. Increased agricultural output prompted industrialization to process food.
    D. Reduced reliance on authority weakened aristocrats' power.

71. How did the Scientific Revolution affect the development of the study of economics?

    A. The emphasis on reason shaped Enlightenment thinking.
    B. The principles of experimentation were applied to economic questions.
    C. The development of new technology prompted the study of economics.
    D. The rejection of classical authority opened a long-forbidden subject.

72. Which of the following is a negative effect of government taxation?

    A. funding needed government services
    B. providing resources for national defense
    C. withdrawing money from circulation
    D. reducing disposable income

Question 73 is based on the following diagram:

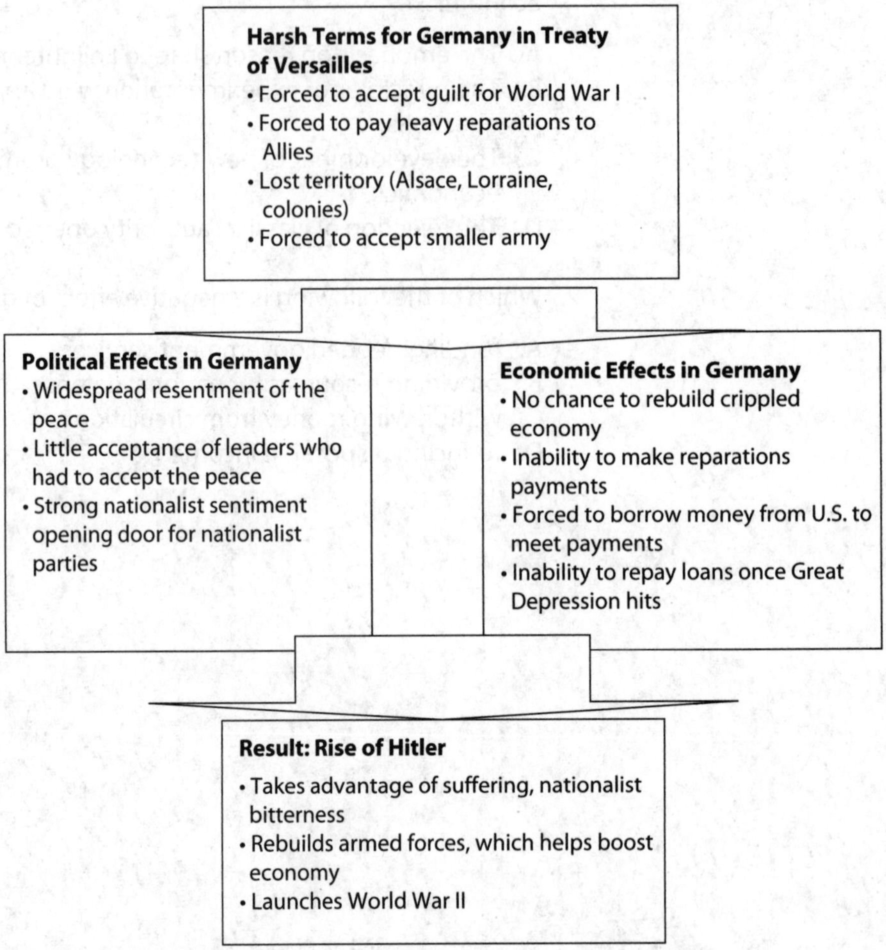

73. According to the diagram, what economic aspect of the Treaty of Versailles, which ended World War I, contributed to economic troubles in Germany?

    A. loss of colonies
    B. the Great Depression
    C. high reparations payments
    D. increased nationalist feeling

74. What was an economic impact of the American Civil War?

    A. greater industrialization of the North
    B. rapid industrialization of the South
    C. entrenchment of the slave economy in the South
    D. expansion of slavery to the West

Question 75 is based on the following graph:

Supply and Demand Curve

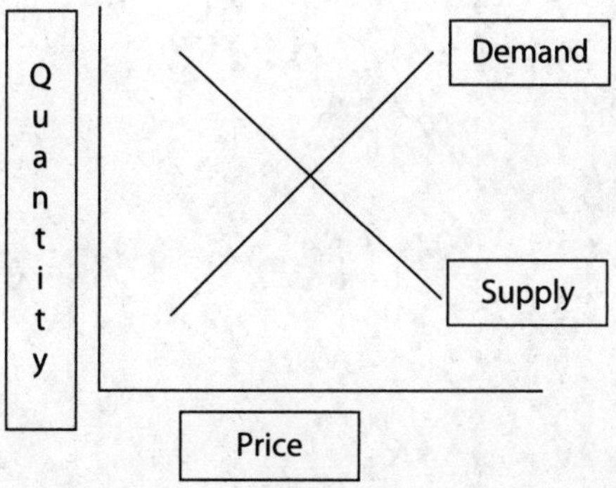

75. Which of the following is an example of how supply affects price?

    A. Three new hospitals have opened in the city while healthcare costs continue to rise.
    B. During World War II, the U.S. government rationed sugar, meat, butter, and other commodities that had become scarce during war time.
    C. An exclusive luxury car must be preordered to the buyer's specifications and can take up to eight weeks to manufacture and deliver.
    D. A bakery produced eight dozen cookies, but an hour before closing only 6.5 dozen had sold. The bakery offered the remaining cookies at half price.

THIS IS THE END OF CHAPTER 3: ECONOMICS.

CHAPTER 4

Geography and the World

Directions: Answer the following questions. For multiple-choice questions, choose the best answer. For other questions, follow the directions preceding the question. Answers begin on page 180.

Questions 1–2 are based on the following quotation:

"A State is an aggregation of free human beings, bound together by common ties, some of which may be called natural, some artificial. The chief natural ties are community of [ethnicity], of language, of religion, of sentiment or historical association, and lastly of land, i.e., of the territory which the State occupies. The most important artificial ties are law, custom, executive government; these are common bonds which the people have gradually developed for themselves and are not, in the same degree as the natural ties, original factors in their cohesion. There are also other ties which do not exactly fall under either of these divisions, such as the common interests of commerce and of self-defense.

Now it is obvious that a State, in order to deserve the name, need not be held together by all these ties at once. Very few, if any, States have realized them all. But every State must have what we call the artificial ties, in some tolerably obvious form; that is, every State must have at least some laws which bind the whole community, and a common government to enforce obedience to those laws. Without these the word State cannot be applied to it, but only some such vague expression as 'nation,' . . . or 'people,' words which in our language do not usually connote governmental cohesion. . . . Nor can any community be called a State which is not wholly independent of every other community."

—William Warde Fowler, *The City-State of the Ancient Greeks and Romans* (1913)

1. Based on Fowler's definition, which of the following would constitute a State?

   A. the Kurdish minority in Iran
   B. Mexico
   C. the United Nations
   D. Washington State

2. Fowler says that a State must have "community of [ethnicity], of language, of religion, of sentiment or historical association, and lastly of land" and that it includes "artificial ties" such as "law, custom, executive government." What aspects of the United States suggest Fowler should have written a broader definition of a State?

   A. separation of Alaska and Hawaii from the rest of the country
   B. geographic diversity of the land
   C. division into state and federal governments
   D. ethnic, language, and religious diversity

Questions 3–5 are based on the following graph:

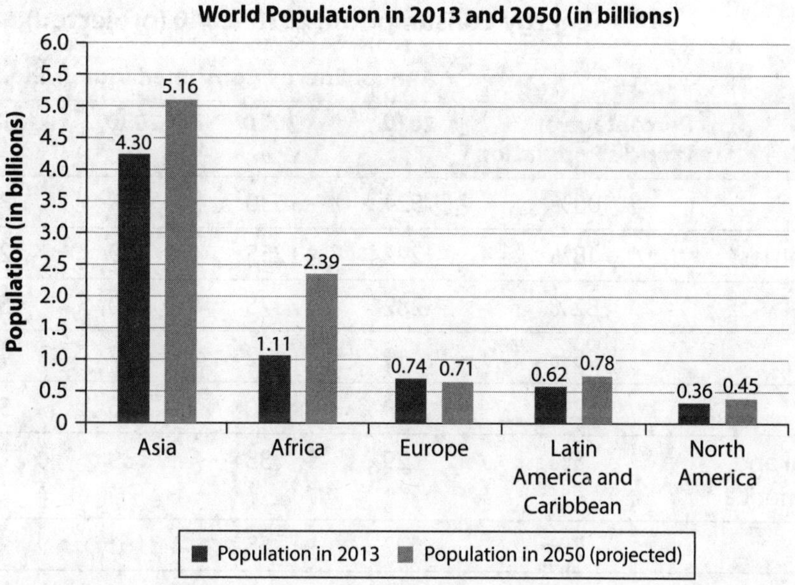

Source: United Nations.

3. Which region is expected to see a population decline from 2013 to 2050?
   A. Asia
   B. Africa
   C. Europe
   D. North America

4. Which region is expected to have its population more than double from 2013 to 2050?
   A. Asia
   B. Africa
   C. Latin America and the Caribbean
   D. North America

5. Based on these population trends, which region will have the most difficulty generating enough jobs for its population in the future? Which region will have the most difficulty finding workers?
   A. Africa; Europe
   B. Europe; Asia
   C. Latin America and the Caribbean; North America
   D. North America; Europe

Questions 6–8 are based on the following chart:

Energy Consumption, 2010–2040 (projected)

		Annual Energy Consumed (quadrillion Btus)				
Region	**Percentage of World's Population**	**2010**	**2020**	**2030**	**2040**	**Average Annual Change (percent)**
World	100%	524	630	729	820	1.5%
OECD Countries*	18%	242	255	269	285	0.5%
Non-OECD	82%	282	375	460	535	2.2%
in Africa	15%	19	22	27	35	2.1%
in Asia	53%	159	230	290	337	2.5%
in Central and South America	5%	29	33	39	47	1.6%
in Europe	7%	47	53	61	67	1.2%
in Middle East	3%	28	37	43	49	1.9%

* OECD stands for the Organisation for Economic Co-Operation and Development and includes most of the major world industrial powers: Australia, Austria, Belgium, Canada, Chile, Czech Republic, Denmark, Estonia, Finland, France, Germany, Greece, Hungary, Iceland, Ireland, Israel, Italy, Japan, Luxembourg, Mexico, the Netherlands, New Zealand, Norway, Poland, Portugal, Slovakia, Slovenia, South Korea, Spain, Sweden, Switzerland, Turkey, United Kingdom, United States.

Source: U.S. Energy Information Administration, *International Energy Outlook 2013*.

6. Which is the best explanation for why the countries of the OECD surpassed all other countries in the world in energy consumption in 2010?

   A. The OECD countries have a large share of the world's population.
   B. The OECD countries use highly efficient energy systems.
   C. The OECD countries have had high rates of economic growth in recent decades.
   D. The OECD countries include most of the large industrial economies.

7. Which region is expected to surpass the OECD in energy consumption in the future, and in what year?

   A. Africa, by 2040
   B. Asia, by 2030
   C. Europe and the Middle East combined, by 2020
   D. Europe, by 2040

8. What is the *best* explanation for why the average annual growth rate of energy consumption is higher among non-OECD countries than among the OECD countries?

   A. They have larger populations, which require more energy.
   B. They are developing their economies faster, which requires energy.
   C. They have the largest and most productive economies.
   D. They have greater reserves of oil and natural gas than OECD countries.

9. Which of the following is the best definition of *sustainability*?

   A. conserving energy and abandoning fossil fuels
   B. keeping an economy at current production levels
   C. using resources carefully to ensure that they are available in the future
   D. maintaining zero population growth to minimize resource use

Questions 10–11 are based on the following map:

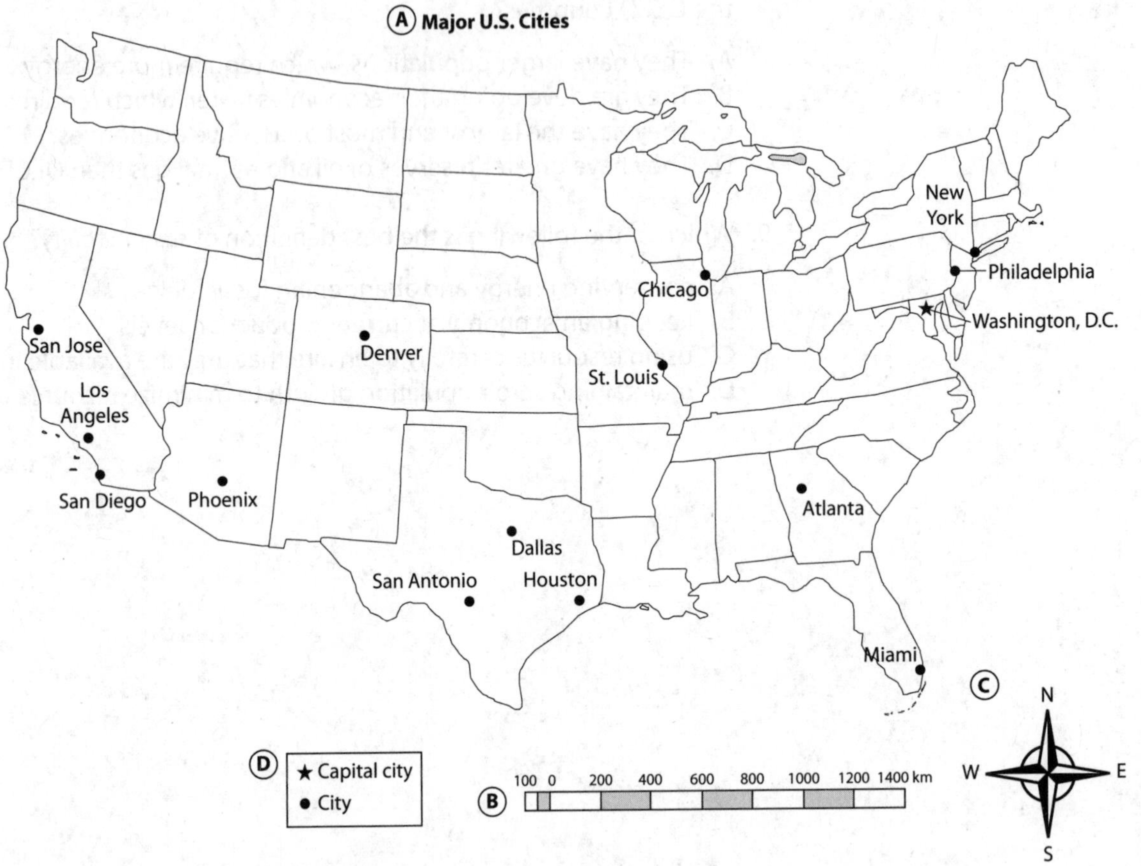

10. What is the purpose of a map title?

    A. to indicate what the map is about
    B. to make it easier to locate the map
    C. to identify the map projection
    D. to identify the area of the map

11. *Indicate the element that shows the scale of the map. (**Note**: On the real GED® test, you will click on the spot on the map you want to indicate.)*

____

____

____

____

Questions 12–13 are based on the following quotation:

"The Purposes of the United Nations are:

1. To maintain international peace and security, and to that end: to take effective collective measures for the prevention and removal of threats to the peace, and for the suppression of acts of aggression or other breaches of the peace, and to bring about by peaceful means, and in conformity with the principles of justice and international law, adjustment or settlement of international disputes or situations which might lead to a breach of the peace;
2. To develop friendly relations among nations based on respect for the principle of equal rights and self-determination of peoples, and to take other appropriate measures to strengthen universal peace;
3. To achieve international co-operation in solving international problems of an economic, social, cultural, or humanitarian character, and in promoting and encouraging respect for human rights and for fundamental freedoms for all without distinction as to race, sex, language, or religion; and
4. To be a centre for harmonizing the actions of nations in the attainment of these common ends."

—United Nations Charter, Article I

12. What is the primary goal of the United Nations?

    A. meeting humanitarian needs in a crisis
    B. providing a forum for nations to state their views
    C. ensuring peaceful relations between nations
    D. promoting economic development and social progress

13. Which phrase in this statement of goals could be used by the United Nations to justify support for the independence movement of an ethnic or religious minority?

    A. "encouraging respect for human rights"
    B. "encouraging respect . . . for fundamental freedoms"
    C. "in conformity with the principles of justice and international law"
    D. "the principle of . . . self-determination of peoples"

Questions 14–16 are based on the following passage:

There are several important themes of geography to consider when studying a region. Location refers to more than just the physical location of the place. We must also ask why it is located there and what is the significance of that location. The theme of place refers to both the physical characteristics of a place and the human characteristics of that place. Region involves characteristics that a place has in common with nearby places and how the characteristics of those places make them different from other places. Movement refers to the movement of people into and out of the place and the effects this movement has had on the character of the place. Finally, we consider human-environment interaction. How does the physical environment shape ways of life in a place and how do humans change the physical environment?

14. What theme of geography is indicated by using a GPS signal on a smartphone?

    A. location
    B. place
    C. region
    D. movement

15. The ethnic makeup of a city as a result of immigration is an example of what themes of geography?

    A. location and region
    B. place and movement
    C. place and region
    D. movement and human-environment interaction

16. Building a dam to provide hydroelectric power is an example of what theme of geography?

    A. location
    B. region
    C. movement
    D. human-environment interaction

Questions 17–18 are based on the following diagrams:

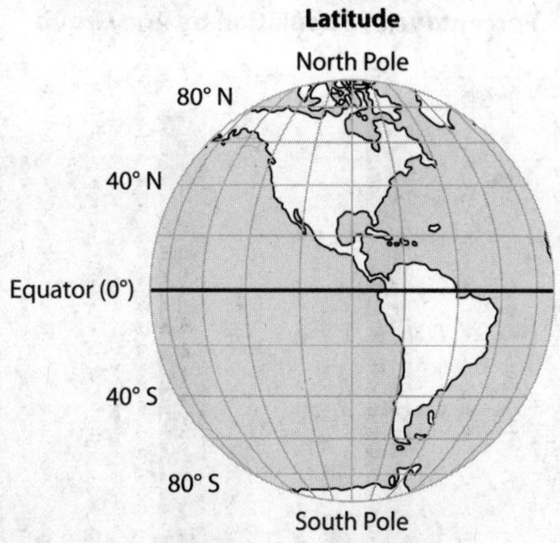

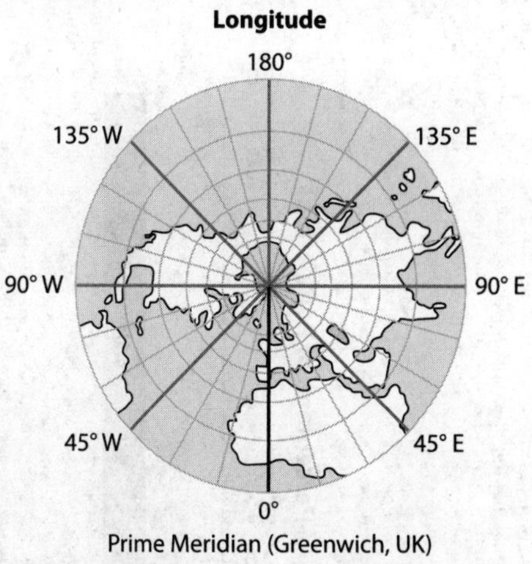

Geographers use latitude and longitude to identify the specific location of places on Earth. The Equator divides Earth into the Northern and Southern Hemispheres. Lines of latitude mark the distance north and south of the Equator. Lines of longitude are used to track distance east and west of a starting point called the Prime Meridian (0° longitude). That line, together with the line at 180° longitude, divide Earth into the Western and Eastern Hemispheres.

17. Geographers use latitude and longitude to determine what kind of location?

    A. absolute location
    B. elevation above sea level
    C. relative location
    D. seasonal location

18. Which of the following continents is in the Western Hemisphere?

    A. Africa
    B. Asia
    C. Europe
    D. South America

Questions 19–20 are based on the following graph:

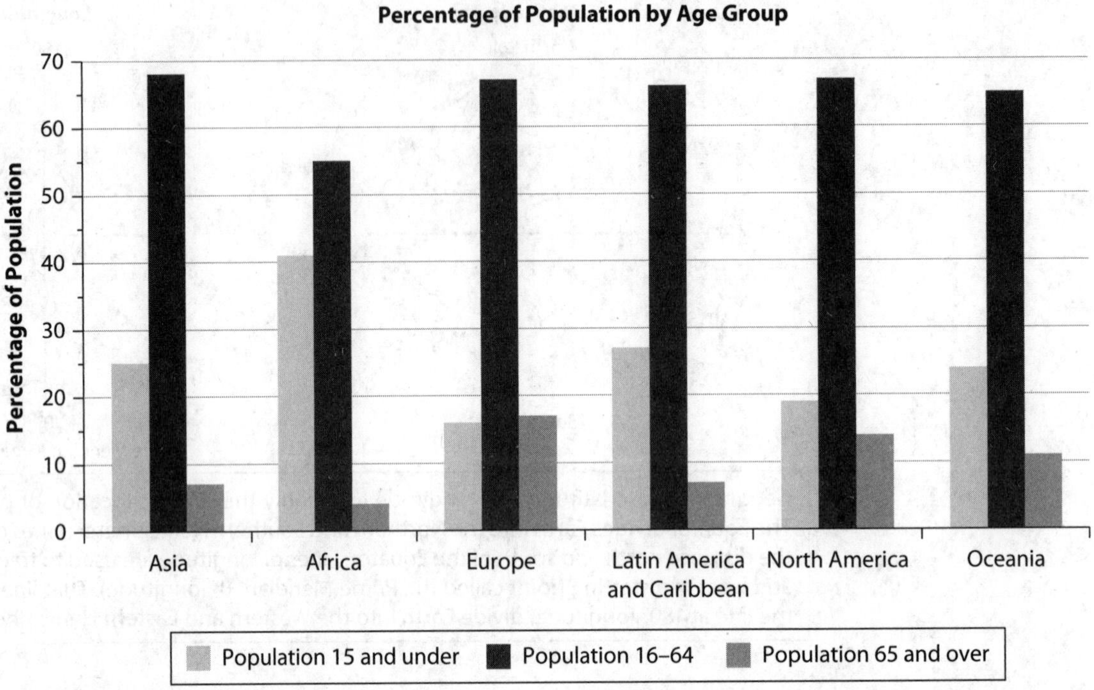

Source: Population Reference Bureau.

19. Which region of the world has the smallest share of its population in the productive working age?

    A. Asia
    B. Africa
    C. Latin America and the Caribbean
    D. Oceania

20. Based on the demographic data, what social issue is more of a concern in Europe and North America than in Asia or Latin America and the Caribbean?

    A. education
    B. housing
    C. elder care
    D. infant mortality

Questions 21–22 are based on the following quotation:

"A Geographic Information System or GIS is a computer system that allows you to map, model, query, and analyze large quantities of data within a single database according to their location. GIS gives you the power to:

- create maps
- integrate information
- visualize scenarios
- present powerful ideas, and
- develop effective solutions

GIS is a tool used by individuals and organizations, schools, governments, and businesses seeking innovative ways to solve their problems. GIS stores information about the world as a collection of layers that can be linked together by a common locational component such as latitude and longitude, a postal zip code, census tract name, or road name. These geographic references allow you to locate features on the earth's surface for analysis of patterns and trends. Dozens of map layers can be arrayed to display information about transportation networks, hydrography, population characteristics, economic activity, and political jurisdictions."

—Environmental Protection Agency, Mid-Atlantic Region

21. Which of the following probably makes use of a GIS?

    A. hand-drawn map giving directions to a friend
    B. smartphone mapping app
    C. map of the Roman Empire
    D. visual directory at a shopping mall

22. What kind of information would *most likely* be helpful to the Environmental Protection Agency?

    A. hydrography of a region
    B. socioeconomic characteristics of a population
    C. ethnic composition of a population
    D. school districts in a region

Questions 23–25 are based on the following graph:

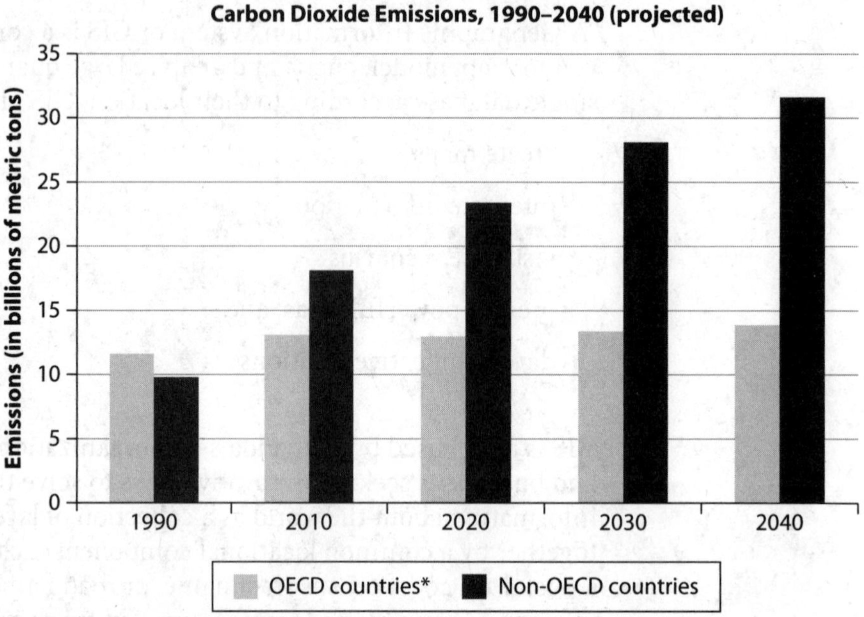

*OECD stands for the Organisation for Economic Co-Operation and Development and includes most of the major world industrial powers: Australia, Austria, Belgium, Canada, Chile, Czech Republic, Denmark, Estonia, Finland, France, Germany, Greece, Hungary, Iceland, Ireland, Israel, Italy, Japan, Luxembourg, Mexico, the Netherlands, New Zealand, Norway, Poland, Portugal, Slovakia, Slovenia, South Korea, Spain, Sweden, Switzerland, Turkey, United Kingdom, United States.

Source: U.S. Energy Information Administration, *International Energy Outlook 2013.*

23. Which statement describes the expected growth of carbon emissions in the OECD countries from 2010 to 2040?
    A. rapid and substantial
    B. relatively modest
    C. marked by sharp rises and falls
    D. generally declining

24. How much are carbon emissions expected to change in the non-OECD countries from 1990 to 2040?
    A. increase minimally
    B. about double
    C. more than triple
    D. increase ten times

25. Scientists urge holding down the growth of carbon emissions because they see a connection between these emissions and what environmental issue?

    A. climate change
    B. water pollution
    C. rising biodiversity
    D. falling sea levels

26. What is meant by a "carbon footprint"?

    A. the pollution that a household or business creates
    B. the pollution caused by fossil fuels
    C. the total carbon emissions of a household or business
    D. the amount of carbohydrates a person consumes

Questions 27–29 are based on the following chart:

Types of Maps

Type	Features	Examples
Political	Political boundaries, such as states (nations) and their subdivisions Capital cities and major cities	• Political map of Asia showing national boundaries and capitals • Political map of Kentucky showing surrounding states, county boundaries, major cities, and county seats
Physical	Major landforms and bodies of water Elevation and depth (distances above and below sea level) Natural vegetation	• Simple physical map: uses colors to show elevations; may use shaded relief for mountains • Topographic map: uses contours to show different elevation levels • Vegetation map of Africa
Climate	Climate zones of Earth or some portion of it May include wind patterns and ocean currents	• Climate map of South Asia, including direction of monsoon winds • Climate map of the United States showing tornado danger zones
Economic	Areas of a continent, region, or state used for various economic activities (agriculture, forestry, mining, and so on) Natural resources	• Land use map of South America • Natural resource map of the western United States
Thematic	Any subject or theme that falls outside the other categories Features depend on subject of map	• Historical: political entities of the past; past movements of people; election maps; battle maps • Population: population density or distribution maps; maps showing migration of peoples; maps showing areas where different groups live • Travel: road or street maps • Many other types

27. What type of map is *most likely* to show and label rivers, lakes, mountain ranges, and plateaus?

A. climate
B. economic
C. physical
D. political

28. What type of map would *most likely* be used to show the location of oil and natural gas deposits?

    A. climate
    B. economic
    C. physical
    D. political

29. A map showing the territorial growth of the United States over time would be what type of map?

    A. economic
    B. physical
    C. political
    D. thematic

Questions 30–32 are based on the following diagram:

U.S. Energy Flow (2013), quadrillion Btu

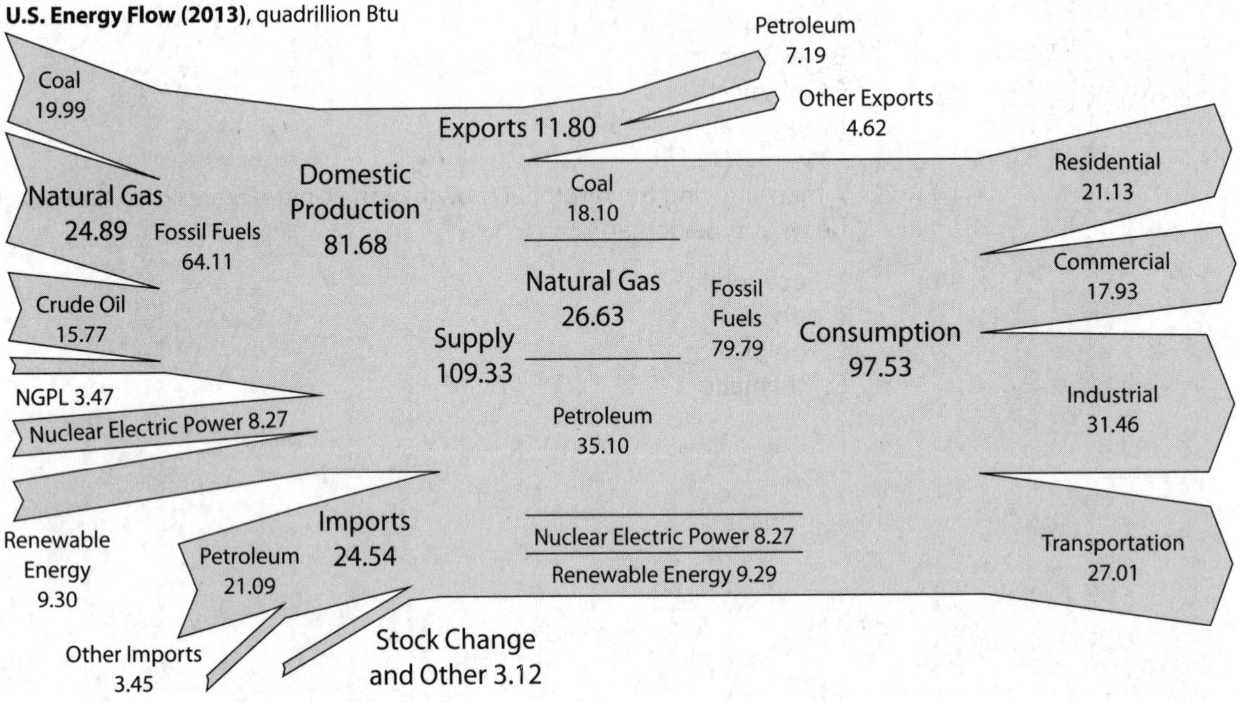

Source: U.S. Energy Information Administration.

30. Fossil fuels form about what percentage of U.S. energy supply and of U.S. energy consumption?
    A. supply: about 50 percent; consumption: about 90 percent
    B. about two-thirds of each
    C. supply: about 90 percent; consumption: about 90 percent
    D. supply: about 65 percent; consumption: about 80 percent

31. What *most likely* accounts for the fact that the percentage of fossil fuels in U.S. consumption is higher than the percentage of fossil fuels in supply?
    A. Fossil fuels are consumed in many different ways.
    B. Energy supplies are falling rapidly.
    C. Most fuel imports are fossil fuels.
    D. Most renewable energy is exported.

32. *The following sentence contains a blank marked* Select... ▼. *Beneath it is a set of choices. Indicate the choice that is correct and belongs in the blank. (**Note:** On the real GED® test, the choices will appear as a "drop-down" menu. When you click on a choice, it will appear in the blank.)*

    Energy supply exceeds energy consumption because some energy is Select... ▼ .

Select... ▼
stored
exported
wasted

33. Which of the following is considered a renewable energy resource?

    A. coal-fired power plants
    B. hydroelectric power
    C. natural gas
    D. nuclear power

34. Which of the following gives the absolute location of a building?

    A. its street address
    B. directions from another building
    C. nearby highway exit
    D. architectural blueprints of the building

35. Which of the following states the relative location of Lagos, Nigeria?

    A. Lagos is at 6° N latitude and 3° E longitude.
    B. Lagos is 114 feet (35 m) above sea level.
    C. Lagos is on the western edge of the Lagos Lagoon, near the coast of the Gulf of Guinea.
    D. Lagos is the capital of Nigeria and has a population of 15 million people in the metropolitan area.

36. *The following sentence contains a blank marked* Select . . . ▼. *Beneath it is a set of choices. Indicate the choice that is correct and belongs in the blank. (**Note:** On the real GED® test, the choices will appear as a "drop-down" menu. When you click on a choice, it will appear in the blank.)*

    The higher the percentage of a country's population living in urban areas, the higher the Select . . . ▼.

Select . . . ▼
crime rate
life expectancy
standard of living
population density

Questions 37–38 are based on the following chart:

Types of Regions

Type	Definition	Example
Formal	Region with clearly defined natural, political, or cultural boundaries	Natural: Rocky Mountains, Gulf Coast Political: the United States, the Eurozone Cultural: Latin America, New England, Chinatown
Functional	Region organized around a central focus (nodal region) or characterized by linkages (network region)	Nodal: broadcast area of a TV station Network: cell phone provider's or cable company's network
Perceptual	Region with an understood definition but not clearly defined boundaries (different people would define the boundaries in different ways)	the South, Midtown, Red Sox Nation

37. *Match each region in the list with its correct type. Indicate the box where each region belongs. (**Note:** On the real GED® test, you will click on each region and "drag" it into the correct box.)*

Africa	downtown	cities an airline flies to
utility's service area	court's jurisdiction	congressional district
pizza delivery area	Midwest	

Formal Region	Functional Region
Perceptual Region	

38. What makes Latin America a cultural region?

A. location in the Western Hemisphere
B. history of settlement by similar ethnic groups
C. similar economies and standards of living
D. similar physical features and climate

Questions 39–40 are based on the following pictogram:

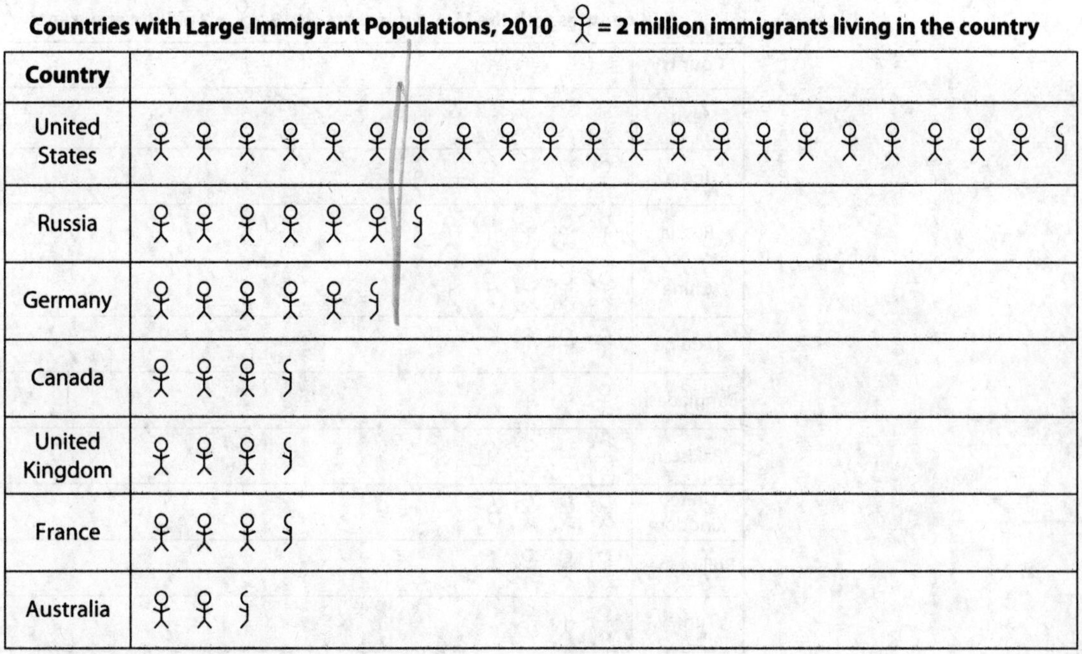

Source: World Bank.

39. According to this pictogram, the United States had about how many more immigrants than Russia, the country with the next highest number?

    A. about 12 million
    B. about 21 million
    C. about 30 million
    D. about 42 million

40. The United States, Canada, the United Kingdom, and Australia all receive large numbers of immigrants. Which feature of these societies *most likely* makes them attractive to immigrants?

    A. climate
    B. economy
    C. English language
    D. membership in the UN

Questions 41–43 are based on the following pictograms:

Countries with the Most Emigrants, 2010 (icon) = 2 million emigrants

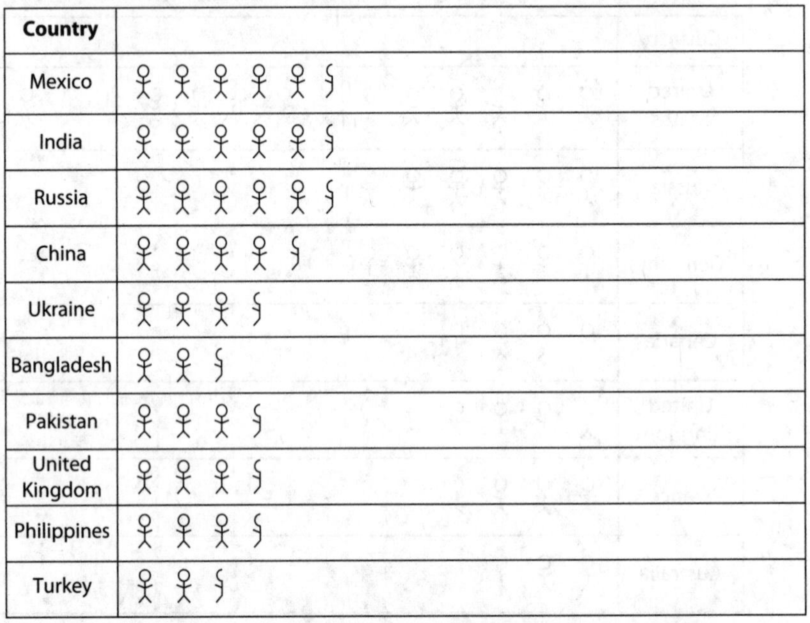

Countries Receiving the Most Remittances, 2010 (icon) = U.S. $2 billion

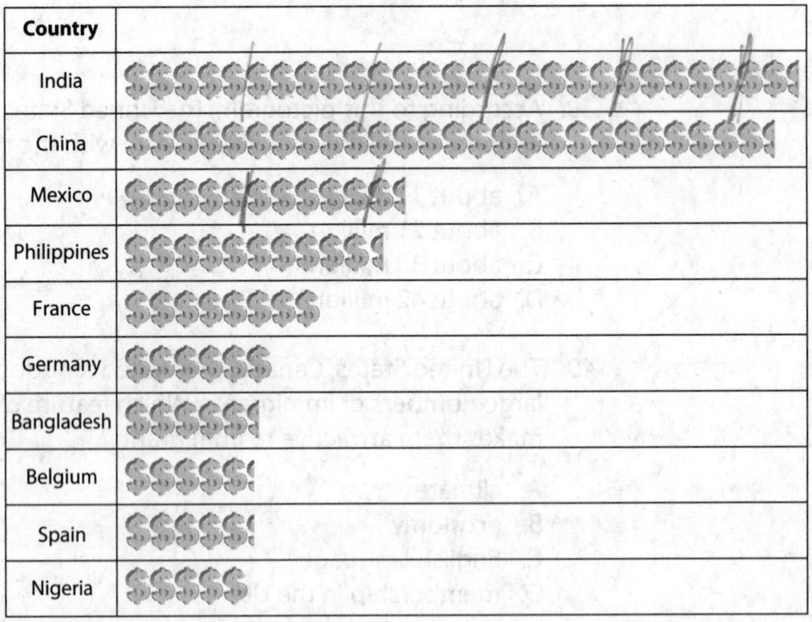

Source: World Bank.

41. Half of the countries that have the highest numbers of emigrants are located on what continent?

    A. Africa
    B. Asia
    C. Europe
    D. North America

42. Remittances are funds that immigrants send back to their home country, generally to family members. How much more in remittances does India receive than Mexico?

    A. about $16 billion
    B. about $32 billion
    C. about $27 billion
    D. about $55 billion

43. Which statement *best* explains why remittances to China exceed those to Mexico even though overall emigration from China is lower than emigration from Mexico?

    A. Chinese emigrants earn more.
    B. Mexican emigrants generally return home.
    C. Chinese emigrants pay fewer taxes.
    D. Mexican emigrants spend all their wages.

44. Why are fossil fuels such as oil, natural gas, and coal considered nonrenewable resources?

    A. They are very costly.
    B. Burning them adds to air pollution.
    C. They are found deep within the Earth.
    D. They take millions of years to be replaced.

45. What is an example of cultural diffusion as a result of immigration?

    A. popularity of ethnic foods in the United States
    B. popularity of Hollywood movies in Europe
    C. adoption of baseball in Japan
    D. accessibility of information through the Internet

46. How do metropolitan areas compare to cities?

    A. They are the original core of the city.
    B. They include surrounding suburbs.
    C. They are parts of the same administrative units.
    D. They include the rural areas that supply food.

47. Which of the following is an example of human changes to the environment?

    A. movement of immigrants
    B. cultural diffusion
    C. building a canal
    D. hunting and gathering lifestyle

48. What is the major factor leading to urbanization in developing countries?

    A. people seeking economic opportunity
    B. rural populations escaping prejudice
    C. migrants fleeing political persecution
    D. urban areas claiming more land

Questions 49–51 are based on the following map:

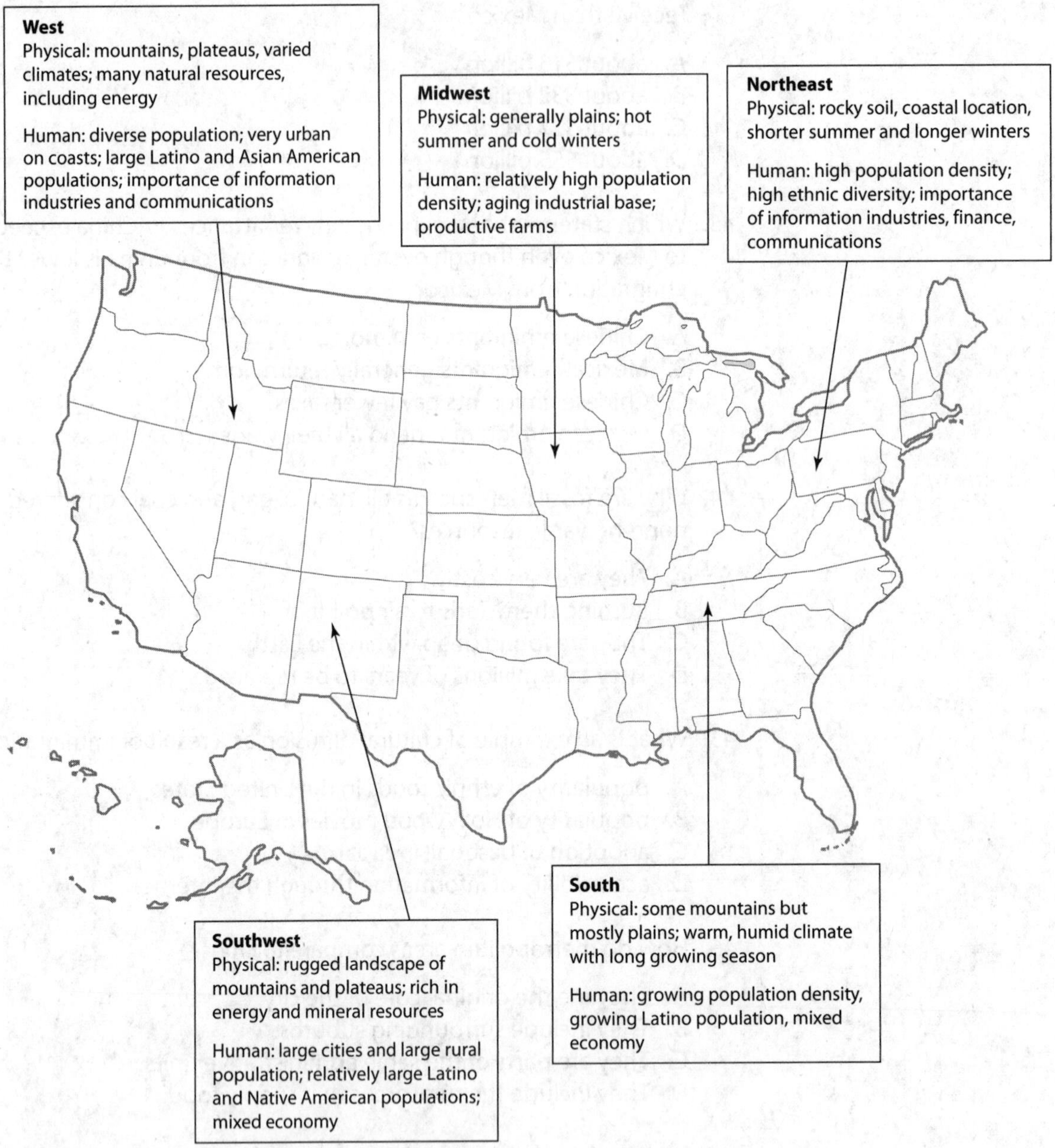

49. The regions of the United States are differentiated on what basis?

A. physical geography and climate
B. history and demographics
C. physical geography and human characteristics
D. economic activity

50. According to the map, what ethnic group is a significant part of the population in the South, Southwest, and West?

    A. African Americans
    B. Asian Americans
    C. Latinos
    D. Native Americans

51. Which region would offer the *best* economic opportunity to both computer programmers and financial planners?

    A. Midwest
    B. Northeast
    C. South
    D. West

52. What term is used to describe the adaptation of an immigrant group to the culture of the dominant society?

    A. assimilation
    B. formalization
    C. migration
    D. urbanization

Questions 53–54 are based on the following passage:

Different tools of geography offer distinct advantages and disadvantages, so it is important to choose the right tool for the job. A globe is a three-dimensional model of Earth. It provides an accurate representation of sizes and shapes of areas and is somewhat flexible in the types of information that can be presented. However, it is not easily portable, and it can show only large parts of Earth, making focus on smaller areas impossible.
A map is a two-dimensional representation of all or part of Earth that is quite flexible in terms of size and format. A map is also very flexible in the types of information that can be presented. A map can represent both large and small areas. The major disadvantage of a map is that it distorts sizes and shapes of areas. Unlike globes and maps, a geographic information system (GIS) relies on technology. A GIS is a computerized system that allows combinations of different kinds of data. A GIS can display a large amount of data and can simulate three-dimensional presentation in computer graphics. One drawback of a GIS is that when using a two-dimensional display, we have the same distortion issues that maps have. A GIS also requires a consistent and accurate input of data.

53. What is the chief advantage of maps over globes?

    A. They are more flexible in many different ways.
    B. They are more portable and easier to use.
    C. They are more accurate than globes.
    D. They can reflect complex data from GISs.

54. Why is it that all maps distort sizes or shapes of the Earth?

    A. They are smaller than the area they depict.
    B. They cannot show as much detail.
    C. They present three-dimensional space in two dimensions.
    D. Illustration programs are not accurate enough.

55. Which of the following is an example of how people use technology to make land more productive for farming?

    A. growing grain on the Great Plains of the United States
    B. terrace farming to grow potatoes in the Andes
    C. producing citrus fruit in Florida
    D. hunting and gathering in a desert area

56. Which of the following is an example of cultural diffusion?

    A. teaching children a native language
    B. recording a folk song
    C. adapting housing to the environment
    D. building a Hindu temple in California

57. Which of the following political entities is *most likely* to include the largest territory and the greatest ethnic diversity?

    A. city-state
    B. colony
    C. empire
    D. nation-state

Questions 58–60 are based on the following chart:

Migration Terminology

Term	Meaning
Asylee	Person seeking refuge in another country to flee persecution in the home country
Chain migration	Characterized by one person migrating and earning enough money to fund the migration of another; the two then combine their earning power to pay for the migration of a third person, and so on
Immigrant	Person who moves from one country to another for temporary or permanent residence
Diaspora	Widespread dispersion of one group to many areas, often involuntarily
Migrant worker	Person who moves from place to place within a country following seasonal work
Refugee	Person fleeing, generally temporarily, an area due to natural disaster, war, or persecution
Sojourner	Immigrant who lives and works in the new home country for a relatively brief period and then returns to his or her native land

58. Which of these types of migrants is *most likely* to come from a religious, ethnic, or political minority?

A. asylee
B. immigrant
C. migrant worker
D. sojourner

59. Which of the following examples of historical migrations is *most likely* characterized as a diaspora?

A. movement of English-speaking colonists to North America in the 1600s and 1700s
B. movement of Germanic peoples from Central Asia to Europe in the classical world
C. movement west of white Americans throughout the 1800s
D. movement of Africans to the Americas in the Atlantic slave trade

60. Which type of migration is *most likely* to result in the creation of an ethnic community in the destination country?

A. asylum seeking
B. chain migration
C. simple immigration
D. sojourner migration

Questions 61–63 are based on the following graphs:

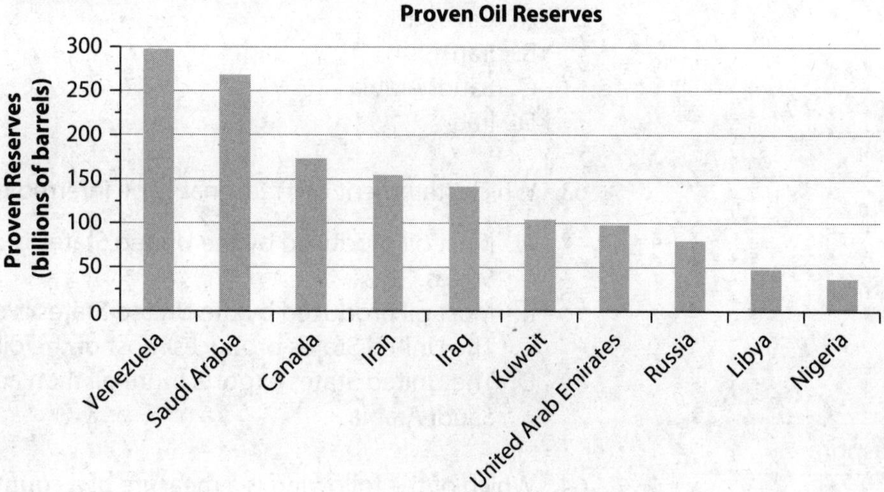

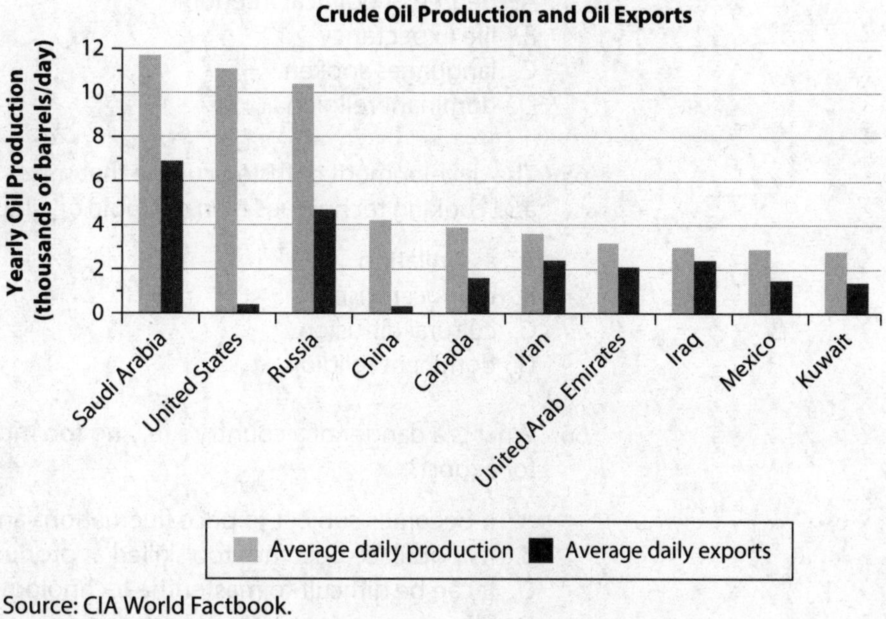

Source: CIA World Factbook.

61. In which region of the world do oil reserves seem to be most concentrated?

    A. Africa
    B. Europe
    C. North America
    D. Southwest Asia

62. Based on a comparison of oil production to oil reserves, which country seems to be making use of its oil in a very conservative manner?

A. Canada
B. Iran
C. Saudi Arabia
D. Iraq

63. Which statement can reasonably be inferred from the second graph?

A. Most oil produced by the United States is consumed in the United States.
B. Most oil produced by the United States is exported.
C. The United States produces most of the oil that it consumes.
D. The United States exports more oil than any other country except Saudi Arabia.

64. Which of the following is a measure of a country's standard of living?

A. degree of political freedom
B. life expectancy
C. languages spoken
D. dominant religion

65. The development of fusion cuisine that mixes European and Asian flavors and cooking techniques is an example of what phenomenon?

A. assimilation
B. ethnocentrism
C. cultural diffusion
D. dominant religion

66. What is a danger of a country's relying too much on one or two products for export?

A. It becomes subject to price fluctuations and reliant on foreign demand.
B. Its populace becomes too skilled at producing the product.
C. It can be difficult to master the technology to produce that product.
D. The climate is not suited to producing the product.

Questions 67–69 are based on the following graph:

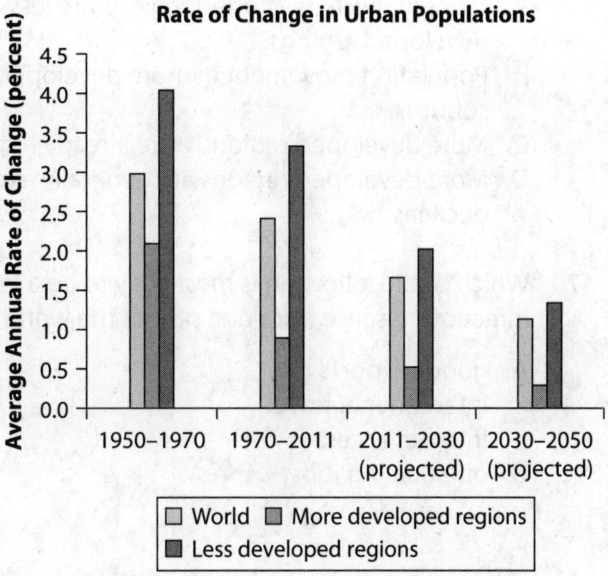

Source: United Nations, *World Urbanization Prospects, The 2011 Revision.*

67. Which category saw the highest growth rate in the periods shown on the graph?
    A. world, 1950–1970
    B. less developed regions, 1950–1970
    C. less developed regions, 1970–2011
    D. more developed regions, 2030–2050

68. Which describes the general change over time shown in the graph?
    A. highest rates of growth for urbanization in less developed regions but declines in all areas over time
    B. highest rates of growth for urbanization in more developed regions but declines in all areas over time
    C. fluctuating rates of growth among both more and less developed regions over time
    D. steady growth of urban populations in less developed regions over time

69. Which generalization explains why rates of urban population growth were less for more developed than less developed regions?

    A. Cities in more developed regions are less attractive than in less developed regions.
    B. Population movement in more developed regions is generally toward suburbs.
    C. More developed regions were already highly urbanized.
    D. More developed regions are generally experiencing population declines.

70. Which of the following is *most likely* to be a factor in the spread of an infectious disease from one part of the world to another?

    A. goods exports
    B. international travel
    C. Internet access
    D. outsourcing jobs

Questions 71–72 are based on the following map:

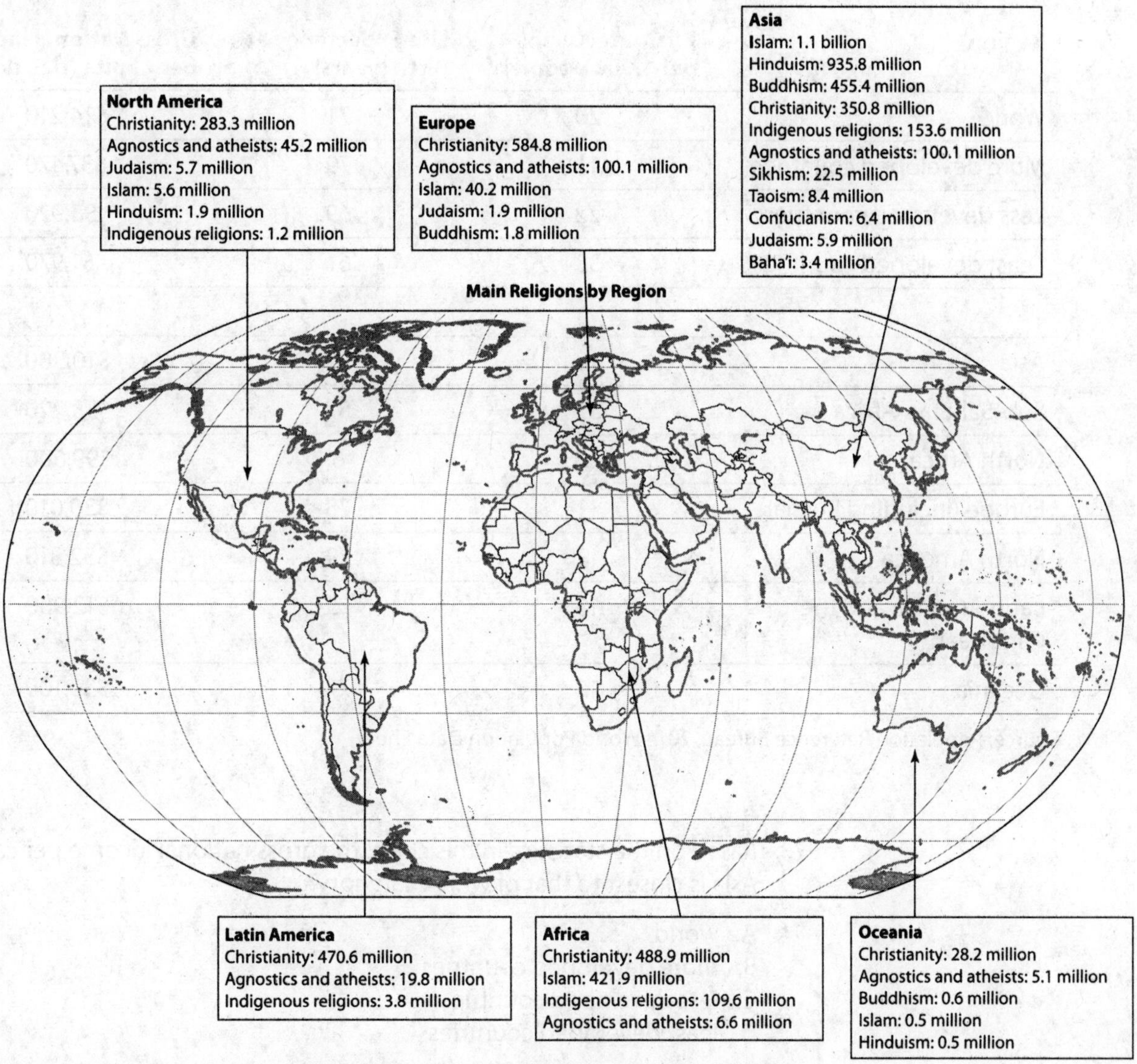

Source: United Nations: World Population Prospects: The 2008 Revision.

71. In terms of number of religions with sizeable numbers of adherents, which region is the most religiously diverse?

    A. Africa
    B. Oceania
    C. Asia
    D. North America

72. What phenomenon does the diversity of religions around the world reflect?

    A. colonialism
    B. cultural diffusion
    C. globalization
    D. technological advances

Questions 73–74 are based on the following chart:

Region	Birthrate (births per 1,000 people)	Life Expectancy at Birth (years)	Gross National Income per Capita (U.S. dollars)
World	20	71	$14,210
More developed countries	11	79	$37,470
Less developed countries	22	69	$8,920
Least developed countries	33	61	$1,970
Asia	18	71	$10,380
Sub-Saharan Africa	37	57	$3,220
North Africa	28	6	$99,600
Europe (including Russia)	11	78	$30,010
North America	12	79	$52,810
Latin America and the Caribbean	18	75	$12,900
Oceania	18	77	$30,100

Source: Population Reference Bureau, 2014 World Population Data Sheet.

73. Based on the statistics in this chart, the gross national income per capita in Asia is closest to that of which category?

A. world
B. more developed countries
C. less developed countries
D. least developed countries

74. Which region is *most likely* to make up a major share of the least developed countries?

A. Latin America and the Caribbean
B. North Africa
C. Oceania
D. Sub-Saharan Africa

Question 75 is based on the following information:

Environmental Protection Agency Recommendations for Reducing Carbon Footprint

1. Reduce energy by using Energy Star lightbulbs and appliances, by maintaining home heating and cooling systems, and by sealing and insulating the home.
2. Conserve energy and resources by reducing waste; reusing materials; and recycling paper, glass, and plastic.
3. Use less energy in travel by walking, biking, or using mass transit when possible; combining trips; and improving fuel efficiency.
4. Use renewable fuels for vehicles such as E85 and biodiesel.

—Environmental Protection Agency

75. Which of the following most significantly reduces an individual's carbon footprint?

    A. switching from driving a gas-powered car to riding a bicycle
    B. replacing traditional lightbulbs in the home with Energy Star lightbulbs
    C. collecting glass and plastic bottles in the neighborhood to recycle
    D. trading in an E85 flex-fuel car for one that uses biodiesel

THIS IS THE END OF CHAPTER 4: GEOGRAPHY AND THE WORLD.

ANSWERS AND EXPLANATIONS

Chapter 1: Civics and Government

1. **A** Locke says that men are naturally free, so this is the philosophy of natural rights.
2. **C** Natural rights are the same as "unalienable rights."
3. Checks by president on other branches include veto power (over the legislative branch) and appointment power (over the judicial branch). Checks on presidential power include the legislature's power of impeachment and the judiciary's power to declare presidential acts as unconstitutional.
4. **B** The delegates were very concerned about limiting the power of the federal government since they had just fought a war to gain independence.
5. **A** The United States has a representative democracy in which the people elect representatives to govern.
6. **D** Direct democracy is when the people rule directly. New England town meetings are an example of this because the whole town may speak and vote on issues.
7. **B** Both federal and state governments must have money to operate, and they have different tasks to accomplish.
8. **D** Canada is a foreign country, so only the federal government may make trade agreements with Canada.
9. **A** Federalism is the system of dividing, or sharing, power.
10. **B** The only duty the Constitution specifies for the vice president is to act as presiding officer of the Senate.
11. **A** The biggest difference is that the British prime minister can disband Parliament. The U.S. president cannot disband Congress.
12. Two-year term: member of the U.S. House; four-year term: president, vice president; six-year term: U.S. senator
13. The president is elected by a majority of electoral votes.
14. **C** Supreme Court justices serve for life.
15. **C** The current debate on gun control is based on the Second Amendment.
16. **B** The Second Amendment specifies that it applies to a "well regulated Militia" and many people today argue that militias are no longer necessary because the United States has armed services and that regular citizens have no need of guns to defend the security of the state.
17. **D** Separation of church and state would prohibit state-run schools from requiring prayer.
18. **A** The court most likely thought that a law prohibiting free expression (in this case cross-burning) is contrary to the First Amendment right to free speech.
19. **C** A researcher who thinks pornography is linked to violence against children might support limiting that type of free speech. The other choices describe people who are actively using their right to free speech.
20. **C** Between 1929 and 1949, there were 885 vetoes, which is by far the most.
21. **A** The number of vetoes jumped dramatically in 1869–1889, and the veto continued to be used at a much higher rate than previously.
22. **C** Considering the number of vetoes and the number overridden by Congress, one can conclude that most vetoes are not overridden. After 1869, the rate is lower

ANSWERS AND EXPLANATIONS

than 10% for every period except 1969–1989, when it was 14%.

23. **B** After 1869, the data becomes widely separated and would be difficult to show on one graph with a single scale.

24. Basic rights: First, Second, Ninth; rights of the accused: Fourth, Fifth, Sixth, Eighth

25. **A** The Fourth Amendment bans unwarranted search and seizure.

26. **D** The Sixth Amendment guarantees the right to legal counsel.

27. **B** The Fourth Amendment bans unwarranted search and seizure.

28. **C** The Fourteenth Amendment granted citizenship to African American males, and the Fifteenth gave them the right to vote.

29. **D** The Twenty-Sixth Amendment gave people ages 18–21 the right to vote.

30. **B** States set their own election rules, but the federal government can set the rules on federal elections.

31. **B** The Nineteenth Amendment, allowing women to vote, impacted roughly 50% of the population.

32. Speaker of the House

33. **D** The rule of law states that no one is exempt from the law, so even the president must obey the law.

34. **C** To override a veto, Congress needs a two-thirds majority in both houses.

35. executive

36. **C** Land management, national parks, fish, and wildlife all fall under the Department of the Interior.

37. **C** This is the principle of popular sovereignty because the people rule.

38. **B** The Preamble states the reasons for the Constitution.

39. **B** Any bill must have approval by both the House and Senate. In addition, a bill cannot become law without either the president's signature or a Congressional override of a presidential veto.

40. **A** If two versions of a bill are approved, it must go to committee for revision to a single version.

41. **B** The number of electoral votes is determined by the number of congressional representatives for each state.

42. **C** Candidates are chosen in primary elections.

43. **B** Article III establishes the judicial branch.

44. **C** The assertion that the Constitution is the "supreme law of the land" is found in Article VI, which lists "supremacy of Constitution and federal laws."

45. **A** Interest groups do not have candidates that run for office (as representatives of their interest groups).

46. governor

47. **B** The Sierra Club is well known for its efforts to protect the environment and promote conservation.

48. **B** The passage says, "a government in which the scheme of representation takes place."

49. **B** The first paragraph describes pure democracy as being for a small number of citizens.

50. **C** The first paragraph says, "There is nothing to check the inducements to sacrifice the weaker party."

51. **D** Congress can stretch its power to "make all Laws which shall be necessary."

ANSWERS AND EXPLANATIONS

52. **B** Preventing discrimination is protecting minority rights.

53. nine

54. vice president; Speaker of the House

55. **A** Conventions are held to determine which candidates will run for president and vice president.

56. **B** Because senators have a six-year term, one-third of the Senate seats are up for election every two years.

57. **B** In 1992, the Reform Party got a significant share of the votes.

58. **D** In 2000, Bush won the electoral vote, but Gore won the popular vote.

59. **D** Oregon, Washington, and Wisconsin were majority Democratic states in all four elections.

60. **D** Texas, North Dakota, and South Dakota were majority Republican states in all four elections.

61. **C** The asterisk says that the other method for proposal has never been used, so every amendment proposed so far has been with approval from two-thirds majorities in the House and Senate.

62. **A** The founding fathers wanted the Constitution to be enduring and strong, but not impossible to change if necessary.

63. **C** Like the United States, Mexico is a republic, with the president as head of the government and chief of state.

64. **D** Saudi Arabia is a monarchy in which the king holds the most power.

65. **B** A theocratic state has a religious leader as its head. Iran has such a leader as chief of state.

66. **C** Article I, Section II, of the Constitution requires that every 10 years a census be taken to determine the number of representatives each state will have in the House of Representatives.

67. **A** The last line of the passage says that larger populations make it less likely that a majority will impose upon the rights of a minority.

68. **C** In the line following the phrase "factious combinations," Madison refers to them as "distinct parties and interests."

69. 435; 100

70. **C** In the first line, the court acknowledges "the importance of the general privilege of confidentiality."

71. **B** The first line of the second paragraph says that withholding this evidence "would cut deeply into the guarantee of due process."

72. **A** The court asserted that the general idea of privilege does not outweigh the guarantee of due process, so the president would have to turn over the subpoenaed documents.

73. **D** The first three items begin with the phrase "Protect the United States."

74. **C** Discrimination is a matter of civil rights.

75. **B** Hackers are committing cyberbased attacks.

76. **sovereignty** Individual states within the United States do not have sovereignty.

77. **territory** A common locality would be a territory.

78 register

79. **B** *Repugnant* means in conflict with, and *void* means not valid.

ANSWERS AND EXPLANATIONS

80. **D** Judicial review is the power to decide whether a law is constitutional.

81. **C** Because the Constitution can be amended, it can change with the needs of the society.

82. **B** Retirement benefits are dependent on age eligibility.

83. **D** Survivors benefits are for minor children whose deceased parent had been receiving retirement benefits.

84. **D** The chart says that the English test is not necessary for some older immigrants.

85. **B** Naturalization is for eligible immigrants who want to become citizens.

86. **D** These are members of the president's staff, so would be under White House Staff.

87. **C** Independent agencies and government corporations would be the most independent.

88. **A** This is the only period shown in which federal employment went down.

89. **C** For most of the period covered, federal employment rose. This likely means that more services were being provided by the federal government.

90. **D** "All men are created equal . . ." comes from the Magna Carta's assertion that no one, including the king, is exempt from the laws.

91. **A** Freedom of religion is protected by the First Amendment.

92. **B** The U.S. Department of Energy, and all other cabinet departments, are a part of the Executive Branch.

93. **B** The decisions differ on what it means to be "equal."

94. New citizens promise to support the laws of the United States, serve in the armed forces if called upon, and renounce allegiance to any foreign country.

95. **A** Researching "biological effects" falls within the mission of the NIH to enhance health and reduce illness.

96. First, someone has an idea for a bill; second, the type of bill is determined; third, the text of the bill is written; fourth, a member of Congress sponsors the bill; fifth, support for the bill is gathered.

97. **A** The Office of Partner Engagement reports to the deputy director.

98. **C** A person must be a resident of New York to vote in New York.

99. **D** Full-time members of police departments are prohibited from serving, even if they wish to serve.

100. **B** A democracy would be most likely to choose a leader through a fair and free election.

Chapter 2: U.S. History

1. **B** The Mayflower Compact was written by the settlers of Plymouth, Massachusetts. It is the first governing document written by colonists in the New World.

2. **A** The colonists pledge to form a "civil body politic" and obey the laws they make together.

ANSWERS AND EXPLANATIONS

3. Choosing the president: electoral college; representation in Congress: Great Compromise; counting enslaved people in population: Three-Fifths Compromise

4. Strengths included the power of Congress to make treaties, to declare war, and to form new states (with populations over 60,000). Weaknesses included the taxation power of Congress, which could not be enforced; the amendment process, which made changing the document very difficult; and the lack of a federal court system.

5. **C** The gray area on the map shows that people were removed from the West Coast. Most of them were interred further toward the interior of the country.

6. **B** President Roosevelt issued the executive order in 1942. Wilson was president during WWI; Truman became president just before the end of WWII; and Eisenhower served after the end of WWII.

7. **B** The removal of Japanese Americans from their homes and relocation to internment camps was similar to the removal of Native Americans from their homes and relocation to reservations.

8. **D** This took place during the War of 1812. It is the only conflict listed that took place between the British and Americans when Washington was the nation's capital.

9. **2007** The only year that the number of employees decreased was 2007, so that is most likely the year it had funding cuts.

10. **C** After September 11, 2001, American increased its efforts to fight terrorism.

11. taxation; crime and punishment

12. **D** The passages are concerned with the rule of law. The final paragraph states this most directly.

13. **C** Clause 20 says that freeman should be punished "according to the degree of the offense."

14. First, Magna Carta; second, the Mayflower Compact; third, the English Bill of Rights; fourth, the Declaration of Independence; fifth, the U.S. Constitution

15. **D** The largest number of immigrants in every single period came from Europe.

16. **C** You can use your calculator to find the exact number (20,773,075) or you can round the numbers: 4.5 million + 3.5 million + 7.5 million + 5 million = 19.5 million. Choice C is closest to that estimate.

17. **C** There was a big drop in immigration from Asia in the period 1880–1889, so that is likely to be when the act was passed.

18. **D** Immigration from Europe grew between 1860 and 1869 and through 1900–1909. After that it dropped significantly. Choice D is the only answer choice after that drop.

19. War of 1812: Britain and United States, 1812–1815; Civil War: North and South, 1861–1865; World War I: Allied and Central Powers, 1914–1918; World War II: United Nations and Axis, 1939–1945.

20. **A** The Great Compromise was between large and small states. It helped establish the system of representation structured in the Constitution.

21. **D** Yugoslavia was a communist country.

22. **D** The United States was a member of NATO; the other countries were not.

23. **B** You can infer that they were not communist countries because there is a different color for those on the map.

ANSWERS AND EXPLANATIONS

24. **A** The first paragraph cites the "laws of nature," and the second paragraph says power is derived from "the consent of the governed."

25. **C** The first paragraph says it has become "necessary for one people to dissolve the political bands which have connected them with another."

26. **C** Italy could not be counted on because it had a secret treaty with France.

27. **A** Austria-Hungary feared the growth of Serbia and Russia was aligned with Serbia.

28. **C** The alliances were so entangled that a local problem spread out to involve many nations.

29. **D** France's assistance was vital to the success of the American Revolution.

30. Thirteenth Amendment: abolition of slavery; Fourteenth Amendment: citizenship for African Americans; Fifteenth Amendment: suffrage for African American males.

31. **A** The first paragraph says, "enough has now been given to party," and the second paragraph mentions "past party dissensions."

32. **D** The last line of the passage says it is America's "manifest destiny to overspread the continent."

33. **D** Nixon is the only president to have resigned.

34. Washington: served as first president, commander of Continental Army, president of Constitutional Convention; Jefferson: wrote Declaration of Independence, made Louisiana Purchase.

35. **C** The last paragraph says the people have warned the British, reminded them, appealed to their sense of justice, and evoked their common ties, and yet the British "have remained deaf to the voice of justice."

36. **D** An usurpation is a wrongful exercise of authority.

37. **A** Nixon lost political support after attempting to cover up his administration's involvement in the burglary at the Democratic National Committee headquarters in the Watergate office complex.

38. **C** After the Civil War, Southern states passed "Black Codes" to restrict the freedom of African Americans. Congress passed the Military Reconstruction Acts of 1867 to divide the South into five military districts.

39. North: growing industry, immigration, high tariffs, free labor, growth of Republican Party, permanency of the Union; South: slave labor, plantation economy, low tariffs, opposition to abolition, states' rights.

40. **B** The country President Truman describes in the third paragraph is communist Russia, and he contrasts it with the United States.

41. **A** The United States followed a policy of containment by helping stop the spread of communism. This is mentioned in the fourth paragraph.

42. **C** This speech was made in 1947, after the end of WWII. The Marshall Plan was enacted in 1948 to rebuild war-torn countries, improve their economies, and prevent the spread of Communism.

43. **D** Harding is establishing "a policy of noninvolvement" known as isolationism.

44. **B** This address was made in 1921, so he must be referring to World War I.

45. **C** The influence of the United Nations is debated because many believe the United States pays too much of the UN's budget and that the UN should not dictate American foreign policy.

ANSWERS AND EXPLANATIONS

46. **B** All of the events listed deal with civil rights.

47. **C** According to the timeline, Letter from a Birmingham Jail was written to argue that "African Americans have a right to push for equality now." One can infer that this was in response to critics arguing that the movement should go slowly.

48. **A** Freedom Summer was a voter registration drive, so that likely contributed to Congress passing the Voting Rights Act.

49. **B** The Berlin Airlift was a response to the Soviet blockade of West Berlin. Western allied nations organized air-drop delivery of supplies to the people of West Berlin.

50. **C** This is known as the Holocaust, or Shoah.

51. **A** Israel was founded to be a safe place for Jewish people, particularly ones who had been displaced by World War II.

52. Segregation: Jim Crow laws, *Plessy v. Ferguson,* Ku Klux Klan; Desegregation: *Brown v. Board of Education,* Civil Rights Act of 1964, NAACP

53. **Illinois** The medium shade of gray represents states in which women could vote for president prior to the passing of the Nineteenth Amendment. Only Choice A (Illinois) is one of those states.

54. **C** Most of the states that had no voting rights for women until the passing of the Nineteenth Amendment (those shaded black) are in the Southeast.

55. **A** Most of the laws relate to the poor and minority groups.

56. **D** In order to staff all these programs, the size of the federal government must have increased.

57. **B** Austria-Hungary annexed Bosnia and Herzegovina in 1908, though the Balkan regions were largely Slavic. Tensions grew due to the Balkans' desire for autonomy.

58. **A** This conflict is over weapons, and Britain and Germany were both major powers.

59. **C** Nations that conquered additional territories could feel more powerful, so their imperialism fed further national pride, which increased the desire for even larger empires.

60. First, Solidarity candidates win elections in Poland; second, the Berlin wall is torn down; third, Boris Yeltsin is elected president of Russia; fourth, Estonia declares independence; fifth, Coup against Gorbachev is defeated.

61. **D** Because the Cold War was primarily a conflict between the United States and the Soviet Union, the dissolution of the Soviet Union ended it.

62. Germany; the United States or the Soviet Union

63. **A** The last line of the chart says that Wilson was unsuccessful in getting the United States to join the League of Nations.

64. **D** Russia experienced a revolution in 1917 that completely changed its style of government from a monarchy to a communist government.

65. **C** Germany had lost a lot of its former territory and was forced to pay reparations.

66. Germany: Hitler, Holocaust, invaded Soviet Union, Nazism; Italy: Fascism, Mussolini, invaded Ethiopia; Soviet Union: U.S. ally in WWII, Stalin, Communism

67. totalitarian

68. **C** The GI Bill was intended to provide returning veterans with aid for education and housing.

69. **B** The Trail of Tears was the forced removal of Native American tribes from their lands.

ANSWERS AND EXPLANATIONS

70. Texas—all the cattle drives shown originate in Texas.

71. **D** Journalists who attacked industry leaders and institutions as corrupt were called "muckrakers."

72. **A** The passage describes sweatshops.

73. **C** The Louisiana Purchase nearly doubled the size of the United States at that time.

74. **D** The period from 1930–1932 shows a significant drop.

75. **C** As U.S. settlers moved west, Native Americans were pushed out of their lands. The map shows a trend of forced removals going from east to west.

Chapter 3: Economics

1. **B** A toll road is a place where the seller of a service meets with buyers.

2. Marina's income is commission, which is based solely on sales.

3. Donna's income is a combination of an hourly wage, which is a guaranteed base salary, plus a productivity bonus, which is an incentive based on output.

4. Gerald works full time for a set weekly salary.

5. **D** Having 55+ companies allows for a lot of competition.

6. **A** The web search market has 2 companies that control 87% of the market.

7. **oligopolies**—the cell phone supplier and the auto manufacturing markets both have limited competition, so they are oligopolies.

8. **B** The Federal Trade Commission must ensure competition.

9. **A** Profit and interest are both extra amounts of money over the base amount.

10. **B** A is price.

11. **C** B is quantity.

12. **D** D is supply.

13. equilibrium price

14. **D** A market is where a supplier (the job seeker) and a buyer (the employer) meet.

15. **B** Entrepreneurship involves taking risk for reward.

16. **D** A tariff is a tax paid on a class of import or export. This is like a sales tax.

17. **2** Physical capital includes machinery.

18. **1** Labor is human physical or mental effort.

19. **D** Antitrust means preventing monopolies.

20. Graph 1 shows a basic supply curve.

21. Graph 3 shows increased production.

22. Graph 6 shows the effect of reduced price on a demand curve.

23. **D** Capital investment typically refers to acquisition of machinery or manufacturing plants that increase productivity.

24. **C** Only choice C involves humans.

25. **D** <u>Wants</u> + limited resources result in scarcity.

26. **D** Wants + limited resources result in <u>scarcity</u>.

27. installment credit

28. **C** Finance charges also include any fees on the loan or credit agreement.

ANSWERS AND EXPLANATIONS

29. Graph 3 shows the effect of lowering tariffs on a supply curve.

30. Graph 2 shows the effect of lowering tariffs on a demand curve.

31. **B** Barriers to entry are low in the dry-cleaning market. There is very little expensive equipment needed and little to no training required for employees.

32. **C** The law of supply states that supply increases as prices increases.

33. **B** The diagram illustrates a circular flow of goods and services.

34. **C** Households own the factors of production (land, labor, and capital).

35. **A** The government also provides services and purchases factors.

36. **D** The government increased spending to create jobs and stimulate the economy.

37. **A** The steam engine was a new source of power that increased productivity.

38. **C** The Federal Reserve Board oversees U.S. monetary policy.

39. **B** Traditional economies use resources efficiently.

40. **C** Command economies have low productivity and efficiency.

41. **D** The U.S. has a mixed economy.

42. **3** Drawing 3 shows a cost (pollution) being imposed on others by a factory's behavior.

43. **B** Government can enact workplace health and safety laws to protect workers when a market may not do so on its own.

44. **C** In a particular area, sports teams have a monopoly. For example, a city typically has only one professional football team.

45. **A** There are many, many types of entertainment, so a sports team is just a small part of the free competition there.

46. **B** The chart says that the Federal Open Market Committee sets national monetary policy.

47. **D** The second point listed in the box for the Federal Reserve Banks says that they regulate banking.

48. **A** Comparative advantage is the ability to carry out one economic activity more efficiently than another.

49. **C** Specialization is the practice of each party producing the goods and services that it is best at.

50. **D** The Truth in Lending Act says what information lenders must disclose.

51. **A** The Equal Credit Opportunity Act bans discrimination.

52. **C** Consumer protection laws, much like health and safety laws, address market failures.

53. **B** Opportunity cost is potential gain that is lost by choosing one alternative rather than another.

54. **2009** The Consumer Price Index rose most sharply between 2009 and 2010.

55. **2008** There is a huge drop in the Consumer Price Index after 2008.

56. **B** Consumer Price Index shows inflation and deflation.

57. **B** The U.S. is at 1.6% and China is at 7.7%. $7.7 \div 1.6 = 4.81$.

58. **A** The largest growth in GDP is for China, Nigeria, Saudi Arabia, and India. These are all newly industrialized nations.

59. **B** The lowest part of the graph after 2001 is around January 2007.

ANSWERS AND EXPLANATIONS

60. **C** The sharpest rise on the graph is just after January 2009.

61. **D** Each country has largely different imports and exports, which shows that their economies are specialized and that they depend upon each other.

62. **B** Japan exports no energy products and imports petroleum, coal, and natural gas.

63. **A** People are only counted as unemployed if they have actively looked for work in the last 4 weeks. If they stopped looking for work, even though they are still unemployed, they are not counted.

64. **A** The chart shows the three categories of bank functions.

65. **C** Banks pay interest to attract depositors.

66. **D** Economic stimulation is primarily done through lending.

67. **B** Two causes are listed: desire for greater share of Asian trade and desire for personal wealth.

68. **D** Both are insured, so risk is low.

69. **A** Comparing the columns for risk and reward shows that greater risk correlates with greater potential for reward.

70. **B** The idea that the universe can be understood and the development of the scientific method led to development of new technology that fueled the Industrial Revolution.

71. **A** The development of political economy is part of the Enlightenment, which was an emphasis on the application of reason and observation.

72. **D** Taxation reduces income that could be spent on consumer goods and services.

73. **C** The box that lists "Economic Effects in Germany" shows that the reparations Germany was supposed to pay were very difficult for the country to accomplish.

74. **A** Industrialization had grown in the North during the war and was able to continue growing after victory.

75. **D** Oversupply led to price reduction.

Chapter 4: Geography and the World

1. **B** Mexico is the only choice that meets the definition. It has a common government and laws.

2. **D** The United States does not have a community of ethnicity, language, or religion.

3. **C** Europe is expected to decline from 0.74 billion to 0.71 billion.

4. **B** Africa is expected to grow from 1.11 billion to 2.39 billion, an increase of more than double.

5. **A** With a population that doubles, Africa will have employment challenges. Europe may have an excess of workers because its population is expected to decline.

6. **D** The footnote for the chart shows that Organisation for Economic Cooperation and Development (OECD) countries include "most of the major world industrial powers."

7. **B** In 2030, Asia is expected to consume 290 quadrillion Btus (British thermal units); and OECD countries, 269 quadrillion Btus.

ANSWERS AND EXPLANATIONS

8. **B** The OECD countries are already industrialized, so their rate of energy use is relatively stable. Many of the non-OECD countries are in the process of industrialization, so their rate of energy use is growing.

9. **C** Sustainability means using resources responsibly so that they are not completely depleted.

10. **A** A map's title explains what the map is about.

11. **B** Feature **B** is the map's scale.

12. **C** Each of the four purposes listed is about peace and cooperation between nations.

13. **D** The second goal involves equal rights and self-determination. That justifies supporting independence.

14. **A** A global positioning system (GPS) shows location.

15. **B** Immigration is the movement of people into a place.

16. **D** Building a dam is a human activity to manipulate the environment.

17. **A** The first sentence in the box says that latitude and longitude are used to determine specific (absolute) location.

18. **D** The globe on the left shows Eastern and Western Hemispheres. The left side of that globe is the Western Hemisphere, and it includes North and South America.

19. **B** Productive working age would be people between 16 and 64 years old. This is shown by the black bars. The shortest of these lines is for Africa.

20. **C** The darker gray shows the percentage of the population over the age of 65. Those bars are tallest for Europe and North America, so that issue would be more important there.

21. **B** A geographic information system (GIS) is a computer mapping system, so it would be most likely to be used on a smartphone mapping app.

22. **A** The Environmental Protection Agency (EPA) is concerned with the health of the environment, and hydrography is the study of bodies of water, so the EPA would most likely be interested in the hydrography of a region.

23. **B** OECD countries are shown in light gray. The growth of emissions between 2012 and 2040 is projected to increase only slightly, remaining below 15 billion metric tons.

24. **C** Non-OECD countries are shown in black. In 1990, carbon dioxide emissions are just below 10 billion metric tons. In 2040, they are projected to be over 30 billion metric tons (more than triple the amount in 1990).

25. **A** Scientists have shown that carbon emissions contribute to climate change.

26. **C** A *carbon footprint* is the amount of carbon emissions of a person, household, company, country, and so on.

27. **C** A physical map shows major landforms and bodies of water.

28. **B** An economic map shows natural resources such as oil and natural gas.

29. **D** In the examples section for a thematic map, a historical map is the first listed.

30. **D** Fossil fuel supply is 64.11 quadrillion Btus, and consumption is 79.79 quadrillion Btus.

31. **C** In order to consume more than the supply, extra imports are needed.

32. **exported** At the top of the chart, exports of 11.80 quadrillion Btus are shown. This accounts for the difference in supply and consumption.

ANSWERS AND EXPLANATIONS

33. **B** Hydroelectric power is renewable since it is power provided by the flow of water through a dam.

34 **A** Absolute location is the location of a place based on a fixed point on earth. A street address meets this definition.

35. **C** Relative location gives the location of a point or place in relation to another point or place. Choice C does this.

36. population density

37. Formal: Africa, court's jurisdiction, congressional district; Functional: cities an airline flies to, utility's service area, pizza delivery area; Perceptual: downtown, Midwest

38. **B** Cultural regions share common characteristics such as language, religion, and customs. Latin America was settled by similar ethnic groups, has similar Romance languages, and has a majority religion (Catholic).

39. **C** The United States had 43 million and Russia had 13 million, a difference of 30 million.

40. **B** Economic incentives provide the biggest pull factors for immigrants.

41. **B** Except for Mexico and the United Kingdom, all the countries listed are in Asia.

42. **B** Mexico receives 55 billion and India receives 23 billion, a difference of 32 billion.

43. **A** Either Chinese emigrants earn more, or they save more to send home.

44. **D** Fossil fuels take millions of years to form, so they are not considered renewable.

45. **A** Cultural diffusion is the spread or blending of different ideas, beliefs, and innovations from one group to another. This includes styles of cooking and popular foods.

46. **B** A metropolitan area includes a city and its surrounding suburban areas.

47. **C** Building a canal alters the environment.

48. **A** Urbanization is nearly always driven by economic opportunities being more available in a city.

49. **C** The map separates regions by physical characteristics and human characteristics.

50. **C** All three regions' boxes list Latinos.

51. **B** The box for the Northeast lists "information industries" and "finance."

52. **A** Assimilation is the process of adapting to the dominant culture.

53. **A** The two-dimensional nature of maps makes them more flexible in size, format, and types of information that can be presented.

54. **C** Maps are two-dimensional, and the Earth is not.

55. **B** Terrace farming is a type of technology used to cultivate sloping, hilly, or mountainous terrain.

56. **D** Building a Hindu temple in California is an example of cultural diffusion of religion.

57. **C** An empire is an extensive group of states or countries under a single supreme authority and can reach all around the world.

58. **A** A person seeking asylum to flee persecution was likely in a minority population in his or her home country.

59. **D** Diasporas are generally involuntary, and the slave trade is an example of that.

60. **B** Chain migration could easily create an ethnic community because each subsequent migrant has a relationship with the person or people who emigrated before.

ANSWERS AND EXPLANATIONS

61. **D** Five of the 10 countries listed are in Southwest Asia: Saudi Arabia, Iran, Iraq, Kuwait, and UAE.

62. **D** Iraq's exports are closest to its production, so it is not using as much as the other countries listed.

63. **A** The United States does not have significant oil reserves, so it can be concluded that it uses most of what it produces.

64. **B** A country's standard of living is often measured by the United Nations' Human Development Index, which includes life expectancy at birth, education, and income per capita.

65. **C** A blending of cultures is cultural diffusion.

66. **A** Too much specialization leaves a country vulnerable to a loss of demand or to price deflation.

67. **B** Less-developed regions grew the most in every period and reached the highest peak from 1950–1970.

68. **A** Less-developed regions grew the most in every period, but that growth is steadily decreasing.

69. **C** Urbanization typically grows with industrial development, so more developed countries are likely already urbanized.

70. **B** The spread of an infectious disease is most dependent on the movement of infected people. International travel increases that movement to a much wider area.

71. **C** Asia has the largest number of different religions listed.

72. **B** Diversity of religion is a type of cultural diffusion.

73. **A** $10,380 is closest to $14,210, the gross national income per capita of the world.

74. **D** Least developed countries will also have low gross national income per capita. The lowest listed is Sub-Saharan Africa.

75. **A** Switching from a gas-powered car to a bicycle (0 emission) reduces carbon emissions more than any other change listed.

POSTTEST

Social Studies

40 questions | **70 minutes**

This Posttest is intended to give you an idea of how ready you are to take the real GED® Social Studies Test. Try to answer every question, in a quiet area and with enough time so that you are free from distractions. The usual time allotted for the test is 70 minutes. Remember that it is more important to think about every question than it is to finish ahead of time. Answers and explanations are at the end of the Posttest.

1. *Indicate the box where each of the following items belongs. (**Note**: On the real GED® test, you will click on the items and "drag" each one into the correct box.)*

two-year term	Speaker presides
tries impeachments	representation based on population
equal representation per state	votes to impeach
six-year term	vice president presides

House	Senate

POSTTEST

Questions 2–3 are based on the following timeline:

1914
June 28: Archduke Franz Ferdinand assassinated in Sarajevo
July 28: Austria-Hungary declares war on Serbia
July 31: Russia announces it is mobilizing army
Aug. 1: Germany declares war on Russia
Aug. 3: Germany declares war on France
Aug. 4: Germany invades Belgium; Britain declares war on Germany
Aug. 6: Austria-Hungary declares war on Russia

1915
Feb. 4: Germany announces use of submarine warfare to block supplies from reaching Britain
May 7: German U-boat sinks passenger ship *Lusitania*; 128 Americans die
Aug. 30: Germany announces it will not sink ships without warning

1916

1917
Jan.: Zimmermann telegram published
Feb. 1: Germany resumes unrestricted submarine warfare
Apr. 6: Woodrow Wilson asks Congress to declare war on Germany
Nov. 7: Vladimir Lenin leads Bolshevik Revolution in Russia
Dec. 3: Bolsheviks sign peace treaty with Germany, withdraw from war

1918
Jan. 8: Wilson outlines his "Fourteen Points" peace plan
Aug. 8: German troops begin retreat from France
Nov. 11: Armistice signed

1919
June 28: German officials sign Versailles Treaty
Aug.–Sep.: Wilson campaigns in U.S. for ratification of Versailles Treaty

1920
Mar. 19: U.S. Senate votes not to ratify Versailles Treaty

2. What is the *best* explanation for the rapid sequence of declarations of war in 1914?

   A. imperialist ambitions of European states
   B. communist expansionism
   C. conflicting sets of alliances
   D. German aggression

3. What led most directly to the U.S. decision to enter the war?

   A. the U.S. alliance with Britain
   B. outrage over the invasion of Belgium
   C. fear that the Bolshevik Revolution would spread
   D. resumption of German submarine attacks

POSTTEST

Questions 4–5 are based on the following chart:

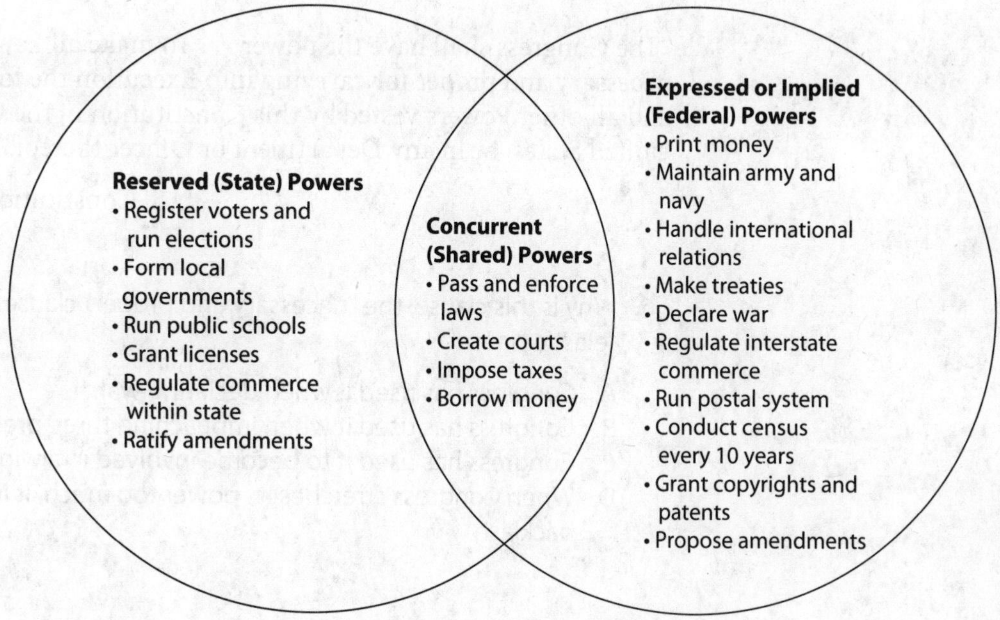

4. Why do both the state and federal governments share such powers as the power to enact laws, enforce laws, and impose taxes?

   A. These are powers all governments must have.
   B. Each level must approve the actions of the other.
   C. Congress passed legislation granting these powers.
   D. All governments aim to enhance their own power.

5. Laws passed by Congress regarding education policy are often controversial. Why is that so?

   A. The laws violate the states' right to establish local governments.
   B. Education is supposed to be a state concern.
   C. The laws interfere with the states' ability to regulate commerce.
   D. Congress imposes rules but does not provide any funds.

POSTTEST

Question 6 is based on the following quotation:

"The Congress shall have the power . . . To make all Laws which shall be necessary and proper for carrying into Execution the foregoing Powers, and all other Powers vested by this Constitution in the Government of the United States, or in any Department or Officer thereof."

—U.S. Constitution, Article I, Section 8

6. Why is this clause, the "necessary and proper" clause, sometimes called the "elastic clause"?

   A. Congress has used it when declaring war.
   B. Congress has used it when impeaching three presidents.
   C. Congress has used it to become involved in a wide range of issues.
   D. When Congress stretches its power too much, it is stung by a public backlash.

POSTTEST

Questions 7–8 are based on the following chart:

Crude Oil and Natural Gas Production, Selected States, 2009

State	Crude Oil (millions of barrels)	Natural Gas (billions of cubic feet)
Alaska	236	397
Arkansas	6	680
California	207	277
Colorado	28	1,499
Kansas	39	354
Kentucky	69	1,549
New Mexico	61	1,383
Oklahoma	67	1,858
Texas	404	6,819
Wyoming	51	2,335

Source: U.S. Bureau of the Census *Statistical Abstract of 2012.*

7. Which state has the most pronounced comparative advantage in both crude oil and natural gas production?

   A. Alaska
   B. California
   C. Texas
   D. Wyoming

8. Which state has the second lowest natural gas production?

   A. Kansas
   B. Alaska
   C. California
   D. Wyoming

POSTTEST

9. *Indicate the box where each of the following items belongs. (**Note**: On the real GED® test, you will click on the items and "drag" each one into the correct box.)*

Bureau of Land Management	Food and Drug Administration
National Institutes of Health	Wage and Hour Division
Occupational Safety & Health Administration	National Park Service
Administration for Children and Families	U.S. Fish and Wildlife Service

Department of Health and Human Services	Department of Labor

Department of the Interior

POSTTEST

Questions 10–11 are based on the following passage:

The Constitution of the United States contains a preamble and seven articles that describe the way the government is structured and how it operates. The first three articles establish the three branches of government and their powers: Legislative (Congress), Executive (office of the President), and Judicial (Federal court system). A system of checks and balances prevents any one of these separate powers from becoming dominant. Articles four through seven describe the relationship of the states to the Federal Government, establish the Constitution as the supreme law of the land, and define the amendment and ratification processes.

Article I assigns the responsibility for making laws to the Legislative Branch (Congress). Congress is divided into two parts, or "Houses," the House of Representatives and the Senate. The bicameral Congress was a compromise between the large states, which wanted representation based on population, and the small ones, which wanted the states to have equal representation.

Article II details the Executive Branch and the offices of the President and Vice President. It lays down rules for electing the President (through the Electoral College), eligibility (must be a natural-born citizen at least 35 years old), and term length. The 12th and 25th Amendments modified some of these rules.

Article III establishes the Judicial Branch with the U.S. Supreme Court as the federal court system's highest court. It specifies that Federal judges be appointed for life unless they commit a serious crime. This article is shorter than Articles I and II. The Federal Convention left much of the work of planning the court system to the First Congress. The 1789 Judiciary Act created the three-tiered court system in place today.

Article IV outlines states' powers in relationship to each other. States have the authority to create and enforce their own laws but must respect and help enforce the laws of other states. Congress may pass Federal laws regarding how states honor other states' laws and records.

Article V explains the amendment process, which is different and more difficult than the process for making laws. When two-thirds of the Senate and two-thirds of the House of Representatives vote to change the Constitution, an amendment goes to the state legislatures for a vote. Alternatively, two-thirds of the state legislatures can submit an application to Congress, and then Congress calls a national convention at which states propose amendments. Three-fourths of the state legislatures or state conventions must vote in favor of an amendment to ratify it.

Article VI states that Federal law is supreme, or higher than, state and local laws. This means that if a state law conflicts with a Federal law, Federal law takes precedence.

Article VII describes the ratification process for the Constitution. It called for special state ratifying conventions. Nine states were required to

POSTTEST

enact the Constitution. Rhode Island became the 13th state to ratify the Constitution in 1790.

Source: Excerpted from archives.gov

[Source: https://www.archives.gov/founding-docs/constitution/what-does-it-say]

10. Which section of the Constitution contains the general procedures by which a bill becomes a law?

    A. Article I
    B. Article II
    C. Article III
    D. Article V

11. Which article of the Constitution would contain the following passage?

    "Full Faith and Credit shall be given in each State to the public Acts, Records, and judicial Proceedings of every other State. And the Congress may by general Laws prescribe the Manner in which such Acts, Records and Proceedings shall be proved, and the Effect thereof."

    A. Article IV
    B. Article V
    C. Article VI
    D. Article VII

POSTTEST

Questions 12–13 are based on the following chart:

		Bank Action	
Depositor	**Amount of Deposit**	**Reserve**	**Loan**
Person A	$100	$10	$90 to Person B
Person B	$90	$9	$81 to Person C
Person C	$81	$8	$73 to Person D
Person D	$73	$7	$66 to Person E
Person E	$66	$7	$59 to Person F
Person F	$59	$6	$53 to Person G
Person G	$53	$5	$48 to Person H
Total in Circulation	$522		

The following sentence contains a blank marked Select . . . ▼ *. Beneath it is a set of choices. Indicate the choice that is correct and belongs in the blank. (**Note**: On the real GED® test, the choices will appear as a "drop-down" menu. When you click on a choice, it will appear in the blank.)*

12. Based on the information in the chart, it can be inferred that the impact of banks' lending money is called the multiplier effect because it multiplies ________________.

Select . . . ▼
the number of depositors
the amount of money in circulation
the amount of debt
banks' profits

13. The percentage of deposits that banks must hold in reserve is set by the Federal Reserve. What would be the effect if the Fed *increased* that percentage?

A. Banks' deposits would increase.
B. Banks' profits would also increase.
C. Banks would have less money to lend.
D. Banks would compete more aggressively for deposits.

POSTTEST

Questions 14–15 are based on the following map:

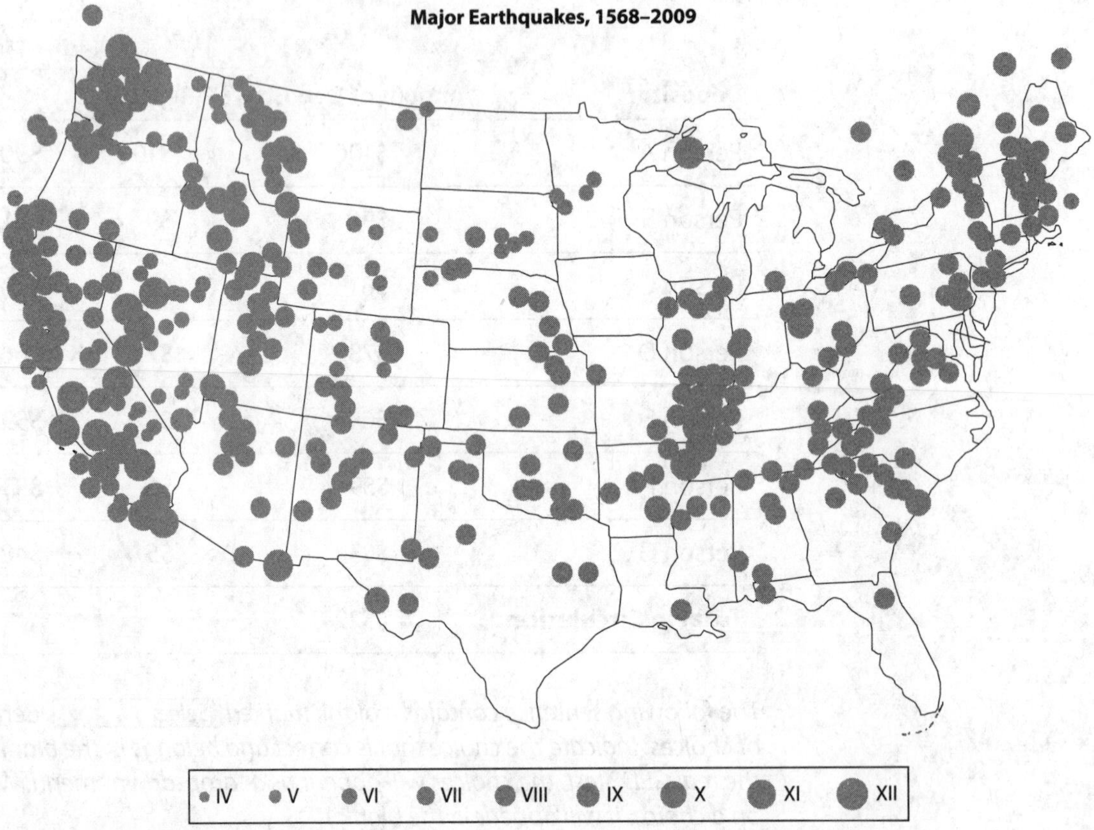

Source: U.S. Geological Survey.

14. Based on the map, which state is *most likely* to experience an earthquake? *Write your answer in the blank.*

____

15. Which area or areas in the eastern half of the nation have the most unstable fault patterns, making them *most likely* to experience earthquakes?

    A. Gulf Coast and Great Lakes regions
    B. central Mississippi River Valley and Appalachian Mountains
    C. New England coast and Ohio River Valley
    D. southeast Atlantic coast and Great Plains

POSTTEST

Questions 16–18 are based on the following chart:

Ten Largest U.S. Cities, 1900–2010

1900	1930	1960	2010
New York, NY	New York, NY	New York, NY	New York, NY
Chicago, IL	Chicago, IL	Chicago, IL	Los Angeles, CA
Philadelphia, PA	Philadelphia, PA	Los Angeles, CA	Chicago, IL
St. Louis, MO	Detroit, MI	Philadelphia, PA	Houston, TX
Boston, MA	Los Angeles, CA	Detroit, MI	Philadelphia, PA
Baltimore, MD	Cleveland, OH	Baltimore, MD	Phoenix, AZ
Cleveland, OH	St. Louis, MO	Houston, TX	San Antonio, TX
Buffalo, NY	Baltimore, MD	Cleveland, OH	San Diego, CA
San Francisco, CA	Boston, MA	Washington, DC	Dallas, TX
Cincinnati, OH	Pittsburgh, PA	St. Louis, MO	San Jose, CA

Source: U.S. Bureau of the Census.

16. What regions dominate the city listings in 1900 and 1930?
    A. Atlantic and Pacific Coasts
    B. Northeast and Midwest
    C. South and West
    D. Southwest and Northeast

17. In which two states are the majority of major cities in 2010?
    A. California and Texas
    B. California and Arizona
    C. New York and California
    D. Texas and New York

18. What general trend can be seen in the changes in the lists of the country's major cities over the period of time shown?
    A. growth of population across all regions
    B. the growing dominance of the Northeast
    C. population shift to the South and West
    D. population growth on the Gulf Coast and in Texas

POSTTEST

Questions 19–21 are based on the following chart:

Major Supreme Court Decisions under Chief Justice John Marshall

Case	Impact
Marbury v. Madison (1803)	Established power of courts to determine whether a federal law was constitutional
Fletcher v. Peck (1810)	Established power of courts to determine whether a state law was constitutional
McCullough v. Maryland (1819)	• Broadly interpreted the power of Congress to act under the "necessary and proper" clause • Established that federal powers were superior to state powers in some matters
Dartmouth College v. Woodward (1819)	Interpreted the extent of congressional power under the contracts clause
Cohens v. Virginia (1821)	Established power of federal courts to take jurisdiction in criminal cases involving state courts when constitutional principles were involved
Gibbons v. Ogden (1824)	• Broadly interpreted the meaning of "commerce" • Established the supremacy of Congress over the states in regulating commerce
Worcester v. Georgia (1832)	Established federal rather than state authority in dealing with Native American tribes
Barron v. Baltimore (1833)	Limited applicability of the Bill of Rights to actions by the federal government and not state governments

19. In which decision did the Marshall Court establish the power of judicial review?

    A. *Gibbons v. Ogden*
    B. *Marbury v. Madison*
    C. *McCullough v. Maryland*
    D. *Worcester v. Georgia*

POSTTEST

20. Read the following passage from one of the Marshall Court's decisions.

"The framers of our Constitution foresaw this state of things and provided for it by declaring the supremacy not only of itself but of the laws made in pursuance of it. The nullity of any act inconsistent with the Constitution is produced by the declaration that the Constitution is supreme law. The appropriate application of that part of the clause which confers the same supremacy on laws and treaties is to such acts of the state legislatures as do not transcend their powers, but though enacted in the execution of acknowledged state powers, interfere with, or are contrary to, the laws of Congress, made in pursuance of the Constitution or some treaty made under the authority of the United States. In every such case, the act of Congress or the treaty is supreme; and the law of the state, though enacted in the exercise of powers not controverted, must yield to it. . . ."

The Court could use this argument to support its decision in which case?

A. *Barron v. Baltimore*
B. *Dartmouth College v. Woodward*
C. *Gibbons v. Ogden*
D. *Marbury v. Madison*

21. In which decision did the Court give a narrow interpretation of the applicability of the Constitution?

A. *Barron v. Baltimore*
B. *Cohens v. Virginia*
C. *Fletcher v. Peck*
D. *Worcester v. Georgia*

POSTTEST

*Questions 22–24 are based on the following graphs. (**Note**: On the real GED® test, you will click on the box you want to indicate.)*

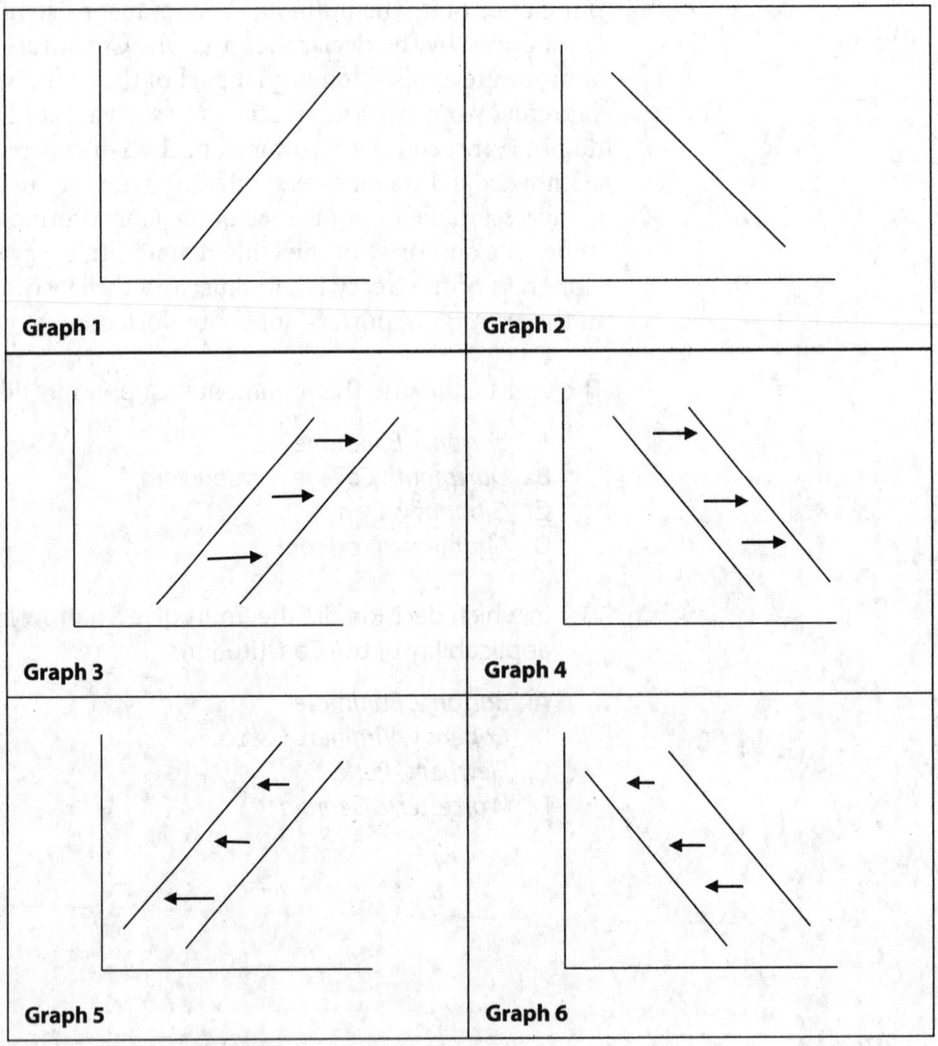

22. *Indicate the graph that shows a simple demand curve.*

____

POSTTEST

23. *Indicate the graph that shows the effect on supply of increased government regulation.*

____

24. *Indicate the graph that shows the effect on demand in a local market of increased employment as a result of the location of a new factory in that market.*

____

25. *Indicate the box where each of the following items belongs. (**Note**: On the real GED® test, you will click on the items and "drag" each one into the correct box.)*

Fourteenth Amendment	Civil Rights Act of 1964
Brown v. Board of Education	desegregation
abolition	Freedmen's Bureau
Martin Luther King Jr.	Andrew Johnson

Civil Rights Movement	Reconstruction

26. Which pair correctly lists the president and a major achievement?

A. Thomas Jefferson and the Louisiana Purchase
B. William McKinley and Reconstruction
C. Franklin D. Roosevelt and the building of the Panama Canal
D. Bill Clinton and the end of the Cold War

POSTTEST

27. Scientists who warn of a connection between climate change and human actions generally point to what practice as the central cause of the problem?

   A. burning of fossil fuels
   B. deforestation
   C. pollution
   D. waste disposal

28. Which of the following are most cited as major problems resulting from climate change?

   A. deforestation and desertification
   B. increased risk of infectious disease and aging population
   C. more extreme weather and rising sea levels
   D. urban overcrowding and crime

29. Which totalitarian leader launched World War II and caused the death of millions of civilians, including six million Jews, in the Holocaust?

   A. Adolf Hitler of Nazi Germany
   B. Benito Mussolini of Fascist Italy
   C. Napoleon Bonaparte of France
   D. Joseph Stalin of the Soviet Union

30. Widespread suffering resulting from what event helped bring about Adolf Hitler's rise to power?

   A. French Revolution
   B. Great Depression
   C. Industrial Revolution
   D. Russian Revolution

POSTTEST

Questions 31–32 are based on the following chart:

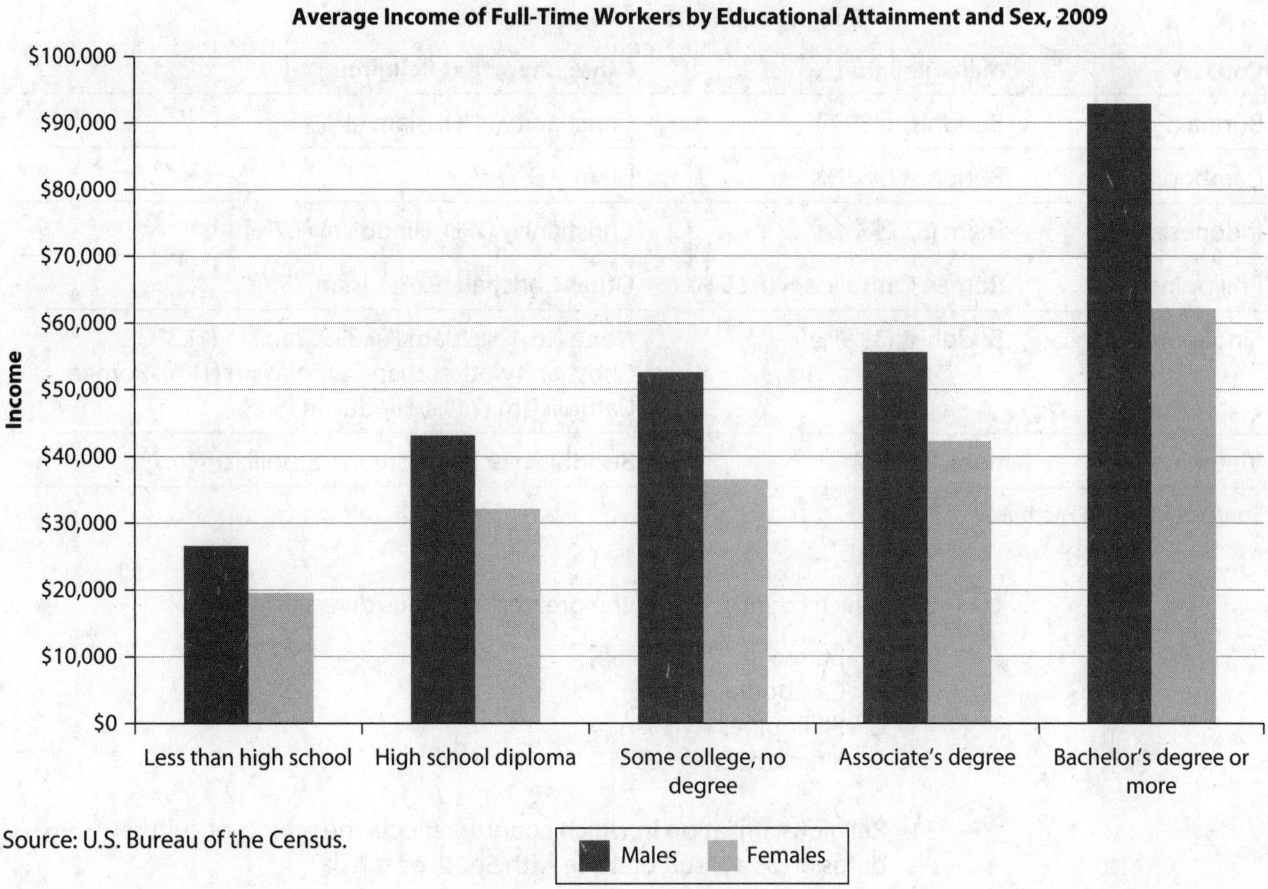

Source: U.S. Bureau of the Census.

31. What is the relationship of income to educational attainment for men and women?

    A. Income rises with education for men but not for women.
    B. Income rises with education at the same rate for men and women.
    C. Income rises with education for men and women.
    D. Income rises with education for women but not for men.

32. What economic principle is demonstrated by this relationship?

    A. the benefit of investing in human capital
    B. the law of supply and demand
    C. the law of diminishing returns
    D. the reason governments address externalities

POSTTEST

Questions 33–35 are based on the following chart:

Religious Affiliation in Southeast Asia

Country	Major Religion	Other Important Religions
Burma	Buddhism (89%)	Christianity (4%), Islam (4%)
Cambodia	Buddhist (96.9%)	Islam (1.9%)
Indonesia	Islam (87.2%)	Christianity (7%), Hinduism (1.7%)
Philippines	Roman Catholicism (82.9%)	Other Christian (9.6%), Islam (5%)
Singapore	Buddhist (33.9%)	None (16.4%), Islam (14.3%), Taoism (11.3%), Christianity other than Catholicism (11%), Roman Catholicism (7.1%), Hinduism (5.2%)
Vietnam	none (80.8%)	Buddhism (9.3%), Roman Catholicism (6.7%)

Source: CIA World Factbook.

33. Which country shows the greatest religious diversity?

    A. Burma
    B. Cambodia
    C. Philippines
    D. Singapore

34. Religious affiliation in which country reflects the effects of cultural diffusion as a result of trade with Southwest Asia?

    A. Burma
    B. Indonesia
    C. Singapore
    D. Vietnam

35. Religious affiliation in which country strongly reflects the effects of cultural diffusion as a result of European colonialism?

    A. Burma
    B. Indonesia
    C. Philippines
    D. Singapore

POSTTEST

Questions 36–38 are based on the following timeline:

1954	*Brown v. Board of Education I:* segregated schools are unconstitutional
1955	*Brown v. Board of Education II:* desegregation of schools must begin "with all deliberate speed"
1958	
1961	*Mapp v. Ohio*: evidence obtained in an illegal search cannot be used in a trial
1962	*Baker v. Carr*: courts had a right to review lawsuits brought by citizens over unequal representation in state legislatures *Engel v. Vitale*: required participation of students in school prayers is unconstitutional
1963	*Gideon v. Wainwright:* state governments must provide legal counsel to defendants who cannot afford their own lawyer
1964	*Escobedo v. Illinois*: the right to counsel applies not only to trials but also during police questioning *Miranda v. Arizona*: police must warn people in custody of their right to remain silent and their right to an attorney *Reynolds v. Sims*: state legislative districts should have relatively equal size to provide equal representation to all citizens
1965	*Griswold v. Connecticut*: people have a fundamental, constitutionally protected right to privacy
1966	
1967	*Loving v. Virginia*: laws banning interracial marriages are unconstitutional
1969	*Tinker v. Des Moines*: high school students have a free speech right to wear to school symbols protesting the Vietnam War
1970	

36. Which cases decided by the Warren Court involved First Amendment rights?

    A. *Baker v. Carr* and *Reynolds v. Sims*
    B. *Engel v. Vitale* and *Tinker v. Des Moines*
    C. *Griswold v. Connecticut* and *Loving v. Virginia*
    D. *Miranda v. Arizona* and *Escobedo v. Illinois*

POSTTEST

37. What area of law was a common subject of the decisions in *Mapp v. Ohio*, *Gideon v. Wainwright*, *Escobedo v. Illinois*, and *Miranda v. Arizona*?

    A. due process in criminal cases
    B. equal rights
    C. equal representation
    D. federal versus state power

38. Read the following quotation from one of the decisions of the Warren Court:

"The right to be heard would be, in many cases, of little avail if it did not comprehend the right to be heard by counsel. Even the intelligent and educated layman has small and sometimes no skill in the science of law. If charged with crime, he is incapable, generally, of determining for himself whether the indictment is good or bad. He is unfamiliar with the rules of evidence. Left without the aid of counsel, he may be put on trial without a proper charge, and convicted upon incompetent evidence, or evidence irrelevant to the issue or otherwise inadmissible. He lacks both the skill and knowledge adequately to prepare his defense, even though he have a perfect one. He requires the guiding hand of counsel at every step in the proceedings against him. Without it, though he be not guilty, he faces the danger of conviction because he does not know how to establish his innocence."

In which case was the Court *most likely* to use these words to explain its decision?

    A. *Escobedo v. Illinois*
    B. *Gideon v. Wainwright*
    C. *Mapp v. Ohio*
    D. *Miranda v. Arizona*

39. Which women were pioneers in the women's suffrage movement?

    A. Betty Friedan and Gloria Steinem
    B. Geraldine Ferraro, Sarah Palin, and Hillary Clinton
    C. Eleanor Roosevelt and Frances Perkins
    D. Elizabeth Cady Stanton, Susan B. Anthony, and Carrie Chapman Catt

POSTTEST

Question 40 is based on the following information:

Europe in the Cold War

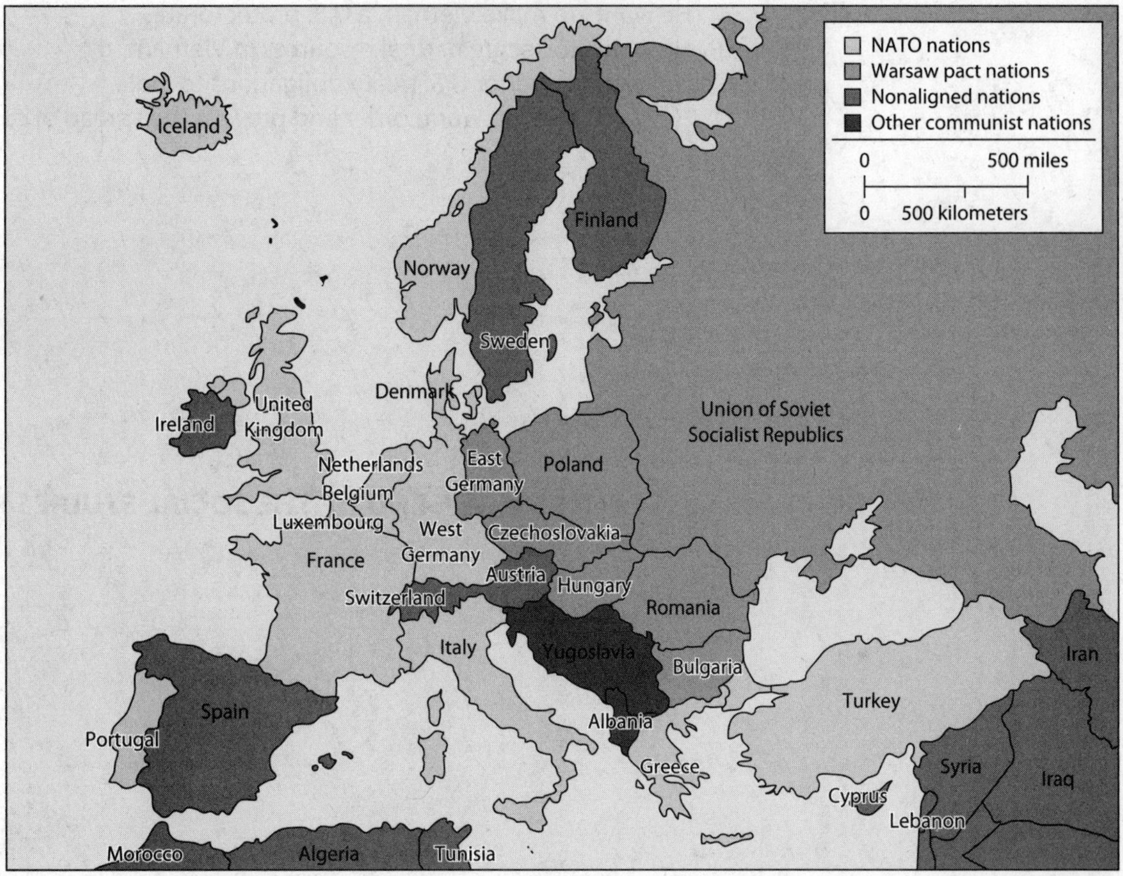

Excerpt from President Johnson's Speech on the Vietnam War (1965)

"North Viet-Nam has attacked the independent nation of South Viet-Nam. Its object is total conquest . . .

"Over this war—and all Asia—is another reality: the deepening shadow of Communist China. The rulers in Hanoi are urged on by Peking. This is a regime which has destroyed freedom in Tibet, which has attacked India, and has been condemned by the United Nations for aggression in Korea. It is a nation which is helping the forces of violence in almost every continent. The contest in Viet-Nam is part of a wider pattern of aggressive purposes."

POSTTEST

40. Which of the following best states President Johnson's reason for seeking to expand U.S. efforts in Vietnam?

    A. He wants to make Vietnam a U.S. protectorate.
    B. He wants to secure natural resources in Vietnam.
    C. He wants to honor U.S. treaty obligations to India.
    D. He wants to keep world order and prevent the spread of communism.

THIS IS THE END OF THE SOCIAL STUDIES POSTTEST.

POSTTEST

Answers and Explanations

1. House: two-year term, Speaker presides, representation based on population, votes to impeach; Senate: tries impeachments, equal representation per state, six-year term, vice president presides.
2. **C** There were numerous conflicting alliances and treaties that required allies to defend each other.
3. **D** In April, the United States declared war. Just before that, in February, German submarines resumed attacks.
4. **A** Any government must be able to enact and enforce laws and levy taxes.
5. **B** "Run public schools" is listed under Reserved (State) Powers.
6. **C** It is called the "elastic clause" because it allows Congress to stretch its powers like elastic.
7. **C** Texas is highest in both categories.
8. **A** Kansas has the second lowest (the lowest is California) with 354 billion cubic feet.
9. Department of Health and Human Services: Food and Drug Administration, National Institutes of Health, Administration for Children and Families; Department of Labor: Wage and Hour Division, Occupational Safety & Health Administration; Department of the Interior: Bureau of Land Management, National Park Service, U.S. Fish and Wildlife Service
10. **A** Article I concerns the legislative branch, which makes laws.
11. **A** Article IV covers recognition of states' laws.
12. **the amount of money in circulation** The loans "multiply" the amount of money in circulation.
13. **C** If the percentage reserved were higher, the percent loaned would be lower.
14. **California** California had the most major earthquakes in this period, so is most likely to have another.
15. **B** The biggest concentration of major earthquakes in the eastern half of the country is near St. Louis, Missouri, in the central Mississippi River Valley. The Appalachian Mountains are another area of high concentration.
16. **B** New York and Philadelphia in the Northeast and Chicago in the Midwest were the largest three cities in 1900 and 1930.
17. **A** Texas and California each have three of the top 10.
18. **C** Cities in the Northeast and Midwest have lost rank to cities in the Southwest and West.
19. **B** *Marbury v. Madison* established the power of courts to determine whether a federal law was constitutional.
20. **C** *Gibbons v. Ogden* established the supremacy of Congress over the states in regulating commerce.
21. **A** *Barron v. Baltimore* limited the applicability of the Bill of Rights.
22. Graph 2 shows a simple demand curve.
23. Graph 5 shows how increased regulation would affect supply.
24. Graph 4 shows the effect new jobs would have on a demand curve for employment.

15

POSTTEST

25. Civil rights movement: Civil Rights Act of 1964, *Brown v. Board of Education,* desegregation, Martin Luther King Jr.; Reconstruction: Fourteenth Amendment, abolition, Freedmen's Bureau, Andrew Johnson

26. **A** Thomas Jefferson was president when the Louisiana Purchase was made.

27. **A** The burning of fossil fuels, which emits carbon dioxide and other greenhouse gases, contributes to climate change.

28. **C** The melting of ice near the poles causes sea levels to rise. This and extreme weather events are major problems for humans.

29. **A** Adolf Hitler led Germany into WWII and perpetrated the Holocaust.

30. **B** WWI destroyed Germany's economy, and the Great Depression hit Germany very hard, ending the Weimar Republic. Hitler and the Nazi Party rose to power, promising a new, strong Germany.

31. **C** Income rises steadily with greater education, for both men and women.

32. **A** Education is a type of investment in human capital.

33. **D** Singapore has several major religions.

34. **B** Hinduism in Indonesia is a result of cultural diffusion from India.

35. **C** Roman Catholicism was brought to the Philippines by Spanish missionaries and colonists.

36. **B** *Engel v. Vitale* and *Tinker v. Des Moines* both involved the First Amendment right to free speech.

37. **A** Each of those cases involved the rights of the accused and due process of law.

38. **B** *Gideon v. Wainwright* involved the right to legal counsel.

39. **D** Elizabeth Cady Stanton, Susan B. Anthony, and Carrie Chapman Catt all were leaders in the women's suffrage movement.

40. **D** Johnson warns about communist China's aggression and says the United States must fight for other nations' self-determinations to ensure our own continuing freedom.

POSTTEST

Evaluation Chart

Circle the number of each question that you missed. To the right of the numbers below, you will find the titles of the chapters that cover the skills you need to solve the problems. More question numbers circled in any row means more attention is needed to sharpen those skills for the GED® Test.

Question Numbers	Chapter
1, 4, 5, 6, 9, 10, 11, 19, 20, 21, 36, 37, 38	Civics and Government
2, 3, 25, 26, 29, 30, 39, 40	U.S. History
7, 8, 12, 13, 22, 23, 24, 31, 32	Economics
14, 15, 16, 17, 18, 27, 28, 33, 34, 35	Geography and the World

If you find you need instruction or more practice before you are ready to take the GED® test, remember that we offer several excellent options:

McGraw-Hill Education Preparation for the GED® Test: This book contains a complete test preparation program with intensive review and practice for the topics tested on the GED®.

McGraw-Hill Education Pre-GED®: This book is a beginner's guide for students who need to develop a solid foundation or refresh basic skills before they embark on formal preparation for the GED® test.

McGraw-Hill Education Short Course for the GED®: This book provides a concise review of all the essential topics on the GED®, with numerous additional practice questions.

Glossary

Important GED® Social Studies Terms

Abolitionists: people who thought that slavery was wrong and should not be allowed in any state

Amendments: changes or additions to the U.S. Constitution

Bankruptcy: legal process in which people or entities who cannot repay creditors may seek relief from some or all of their debts

Bill of Rights: the first ten amendments to the U.S. Constitution; they place restrictions on the government's power and guarantee certain rights and civil liberties to the citizens

Bond: a loan to a company or government that pays the investor a fixed rate of return over a specific length of time

Cabinet: a group whose role is to advise the president on subjects related to each member's office; includes Vice President, Attorney General, and the heads of the executive departments

Capital: assets used to finance a business, including money, buildings, or equipment

Civil Rights movement: mass protest movement beginning in 1954 against racial segregation and discrimination in the United States

Climate: the pattern of weather in a particular region, including prevailing winds, temperatures, and the amount and type of precipitation, averaged over time

Cold War: the period from 1945 to 1990 in which Soviet countries and the United States and its allies existed in a state of political hostility

Colonialism: policy of a country seeking to extend its authority over other people or territories

Comparative advantage: greater profit for a business that can produce a good at a lower cost than any other business can

Conservatism: political and social philosophy promoting traditional social institutions

Credit: an arrangement that allows consumers to finance a purchase without having to pay the total cost at the time the purchase is made

Cultural diffusion: the spread of cultural ideas to new groups of people

Debt: an amount of money borrowed by one party (the debtor) from another party (the creditor)

Declaration of Independence: document in which the 13 American colonies declared independence from England and stated principles for forming their new government

Deflation: a general reduction of prices in an economy

Demand: the amount of an item that consumers wish to purchase

Democracy: type of government in which citizens exercise power, either directly or through representatives

Diaspora: the scattering of groups of people that have been dispersed outside of their homelands either by choice or involuntarily

Dictatorship: a type of government in which a single leader exercises absolute power over nearly every aspect of life in a country, including political, social, and economic issues

Dust Bowl: a nickname given to the Southern Plains region of the United States, which suffered severe *dust storms* during a long period of drought in the 1930s

Economics: study of the continuous exchange of goods, services, and resources in society

Ecosystem: the ongoing interaction between the land, climate, and living organisms in a particular location

Elastic clause: allows the U.S. Congress to stretch its powers to fit specific situations as needed

Electoral College: formal body of electors that actually elects the president of the United States

Embargo: official ban on commercial activity with another country in order to apply pressure

Emigrate: to leave a country in order to settle in another place

Enlightenment: 18th-century period in which philosophers applied the scientific process of critical thinking to social and political problems

Entrepreneurship: the quality of being an entrepreneur, someone who owns and manages a business and therefore shoulders the risk and effort involved in running that business

Equilibrium: in economics, the price at which supply and demand for an item are balanced

Export: selling goods and services produced in the home country to other markets

Fascism: nationalistic political philosophy that stands for a centralized autocratic government led by a dictator, economic and social regimentation, and forcible suppression of opposition

Federalism: the principle of separation of powers and functions between the federal government and the governments of the states

Fertile Crescent: area in present-day Iraq, Syria, and Egypt that was home to early civilizations

Feudalism: social system in which people work and fight for nobles who give them protection and land; common in medieval Europe

Fiscal policy: to the way in which government collects and spends tax revenues

GI Bill: 1944 bill that provided benefits to veterans to help them transition back into civilian life

Global warming: the rising average temperature of Earth's climate system

Great Depression: a serious worldwide economic depression that began with the crash of the U.S. stock market in October 1929 and lasted through most of the 1930s

Great Society: U.S. President Johnson's plan to eliminate poverty

Gross domestic product (GDP): the total dollar value of all the goods and services produced by a country over a specific time period

Holocaust: Nazi racial persecution and genocide of European Jews during WWII

Immigrate: to move into a country, usually to establish permanent residence

Import: goods and services brought into the home country from an exterior source

Industrial Revolution: 18th-century period transition from rural, agrarian economies to urban economies dominated by industry and machine manufacturing

Inflation: a general, ongoing rise in the prices of goods and services

Interest: fee paid for the privilege of borrowing money, typically given as a percentage rate

Interest groups: groups of people who share a common interest or concern who come together to influence the government

Investment: item that is purchased in the hope that it will become more valuable in the future

Iron Curtain: nickname for the political border between Western and Eastern Europe from the late 1940s until 1989

Judicial review: the responsibility of the U.S. Supreme Court to determine whether laws are constitutional

Labor: workers and the work they do, both mental and physical

Latitude and longitude: a geographic coordinate system through which the position or location of any place on Earth's surface can be determined

League of Nations: an international organization formed after WWI to settle differences between nations through diplomacy rather than war

Liberalism: political and moral philosophy based on constitutional government, equality of legal rights, and free enterprise

Macroeconomics: the study of the overall workings of a national economy and of its relationship to international markets

Magna Carta: 1215 English document that established key rights, such as the right to a representative government with powers over taxation, the right to trial by jury, and the right to due process in legal matters; influenced Declaration of Independence

Manifest destiny: the belief that the United States was "destined" to occupy the entire North American continent, from the Atlantic Ocean to the Pacific Ocean

Market: any place where the seller of a particular good or service can meet with buyers

Marshall Plan: a plan to help rebuild Europe after WWII in order to provide political stability and help the world economy

Marxism: philosophy developed by Karl Marx and Friedrich Engels that states that the working class should overthrow the capitalist system through an international revolution

Microeconomics: the study of individual markets

Migration: movement of large numbers of people from one country, place, or region to another

Monarchy: a political system in which power is held by a king, a queen, an emperor, or an empress who generally rules until the end of his or her life and then passes leadership on to his or her heirs

Monetary policy: relates to the supply of money, which is controlled by factors such as interest rates and reserve requirements for banks

Monopoly: when a seller is the only one to offer a certain good or service

Monroe Doctrine: U.S. foreign policy to resist any effort by European countries to attack or establish new colonies in North or South America and to remain neutral in any European conflicts; introduced the United States as a player in world politics

Nationalism: pride in one's ethnic, cultural, and linguistic heritage, often to the exclusion or detriment of the interests of others

NATO (North Atlantic Treaty Organization): a military alliance between the United States and its European allies to counter the Soviet threat

Natural resources: materials or substances occurring in nature used for economic gain

Natural rights: the idea that individuals have certain rights just because they are human beings

New Deal: U.S. President Franklin Roosevelt's programs to create millions of jobs and restore the nation's banks to a sound financial footing

Oligarchy: political system in which power is held by a small group of people not elected by the citizens, usually members of an upper class

Opportunity cost: gains that are passed over in the choice of doing one thing instead of another

Political parties: organizations that seek power and influence within the government and are generally made up of members who share similar opinions and ideas about many issues

Popular sovereignty: principle that government derives its power from the consent of the governed and that the people have the right to a voice in deciding how decisions are reached

Primary elections: candidates from the same political party run for the same office against one another to determine which one will be the party's nominee in the general election

Productivity: output per unit of labor, or the rate at which goods or services are produced

Profit: excess capital earned when a good is sold for more than it cost to produce

Reconstruction: period in U.S. history from 1865 to 1877 in which efforts were made to allow the former Confederate states to rejoin the Union and to integrate African Americans

Reformation: religious movement to challenge the Catholic church that began in 1517 with the founding of the Lutheran Church

Renaissance: 1350–1600 European cultural revival characterized by a sharp rise in literacy and a resurgence of interest in Classical philosophy, literature, and art

Scientific Revolution: 1543–1687 period that featured great progress in human understanding of the laws of the universe

Segregation: post-slavery system of legal separation of the races in the United States that began to be overturned in 1954 with *Brown v. Board of Education*

Separation of powers/system of checks and balances: the U.S. Constitution divides the federal government into three branches and each branch checks the power of the other two

Silk Road: major overland trade route from China to Constantinople and Alexandria

Socialism: political philosophy based on the idea that government control of the economy can reduce or eradicate social injustice

Specialization: focusing on a limited area of economic activity

Stocks: stakes of ownership in a company

Supply: the amount of a good that is available

Surplus: an excess of production

Tariffs: taxes or duties paid on specified classes of imports or exports

Tax: a compulsory financial charge imposed by a governmental organization

Topography: the physical features of the land

Trail of Tears: U.S. government's forced removal of Cherokee from their lands east of the Mississippi River to an area in present-day Oklahoma during which one-fourth died

Truman Doctrine: an American foreign policy established in 1947 that promised to help democratic nations threatened by Communism

Wages: the money workers earn from their labor

War on Terror: global counterterrorism military campaign started by the United States after the September 11 attacks

Watergate: American political scandal in 1972 that led to Nixon's resignation